the book of
PSALMS
ספר תהלים

THE BOOK OF
PSALMS
ספר תהלים

A New Translation
According to the Traditional
Hebrew Text

The Jewish Publication Society

© 1972 by The Jewish Publication Society
First edition, second printing 1975
Revised edition with updated translation 1997

Manufactured in the United States of America

Library of Congress Cataloging-in-Publication Data

Bible. O.T. Psalms. English. Jewish Publication Society. 1997.
    The book of Psalms=Sefer Tehilim: a new translation according to
the traditional Hebrew text.
    p. cm.
Previously published: Philadelphia: Jewish Publication Society of
America, 1972. With additional material.

    ISBN 0-8276-0630-3 (case). – ISBN 0-8276-0631-1 (paper)
    I. Jewish Publication Society of America. II. Title.
BS1422 1997
223' .205208–dc21

97-6261
CIP
r97

In 1966 the Jewish Publication Society set up a committee of translators for the Ketubim, comprising professors Moshe Greenberg of the University of Pennsylvania (now of the Hebrew University), Jonas C. Greenfield of the University of California (now of the Hebrew University), and Nahum M. Sarna of Brandeis University, and associated with them rabbis Saul Leeman, Martin Rozenberg, and David Shapiro of the three sections of organized religious Jewish life in America. Dr. Chaim Potok, editor of the Society, served as secretary of the committee.

This English rendering of Psalms, the committee's first work, is a new version, not a revision of an earlier translation. It is based on the received (Masoretic) Hebrew text—its consonants, vowels, and syntactical divisions, although on occasion the traditional accentuation has been disregarded in favor of an alternative construction of a verse that appeared to yield a better sense. Such departures from the accentuation were made by many earlier Jewish commentators and translators.

The entire gamut of Psalms interpretation, from ancient to modern times, Jewish and non-Jewish, has been consulted. The results of modern study of the languages and cultures of the ancient Near East have been brought to bear on the biblical word wherever possible. In judging between alternatives, however, just as antiquity was not in itself a disqualification, so modernity was not in itself a recommendation. When the present translation diverges from recent renderings (as it frequently does), this is due as much to the committee's judgment that certain innovations, though interesting, are too speculative for adoption in the present state of knowledge, as to its commitment to the received Hebrew text (a commitment not made by most recent translations).

For many passages, our as yet imperfect understanding of the language of the Bible or what appears to be some disorder in the Hebrew text makes sure translation impossible. The committee's uncertainty is indicated in a marginal note, and alternative renderings have sometimes been offered where the Hebrew permits them. However, emendations of the text have not been proposed.

The style of the translation is, on the whole, modern literary English. An effort has been made to retain the imagery of the Hebrew rather than to render it by English equivalents and approximations alien to the biblical world.

Consistency in rendering Hebrew terms was an aim but not an unqualified rule. Where its employment would have resulted in encumbered or awkward language it was abandoned. On the other hand, within a given psalm, key or thematic words and phrases were, as far as possible, rendered consistently. Repetition of key or thematic terms is an element of structure and composition in the psalms; its representation is one of the proper tasks of a translator. Terms having many values, such as ḥesed and ṣedeq (in the King James version, "mercy/lovingkindness" and "righteousness") posed a problem. In order to do justice to their wide range, a variety of renderings determined by the various contexts had to be employed. Here consistency was neither possible nor desirable.

The translators know that they have not conveyed the fullness of the Hebrew, with its ambiguities, its overtones, and the richness of meaning it carries from centuries of use. They do hope to have transmitted something of the directness, the simplicity, and the peculiarly Israelite expression of piety that are so essential to the sublimity of the Hebrew psalms.

ספר
תהלים

THE BOOK OF
PSALMS

תהילים

PSALMS

BOOK ONE

1

Happy is the man who has not followed the counsel of the
    wicked,
    or taken the path of sinners,
    or joined the company of the insolent;
    [2]rather, the teaching of the LORD is his delight,
    and he studies[a] that teaching day and night.
    [3]He is like a tree planted beside streams of water,
    which yields its fruit in season,
    whose foliage never fades,
    and whatever [b]it produces thrives.[-b]

[4]Not so the wicked;
    rather, they are like chaff that wind blows away.
[5]Therefore the wicked will not survive judgment,
    nor will sinners, in the assembly of the righteous.
[6]For the LORD cherishes the way of the righteous,
    but the way of the wicked is doomed.

2

Why do nations assemble,
    and peoples plot[a] vain things;
    [2]kings of the earth take their stand,
    and regents intrigue together
    against the LORD and against His anointed?
    [3]"Let us break the cords of their yoke,
    shake off their ropes from us!"

---

[a] Or "recites"; lit. "utters."
[b-b] Or "he does prospers."

[a] Lit. "utter."

⁴He who is enthroned in heaven laughs;
   the Lord mocks at them.
⁵Then He speaks to them in anger,
   terrifying them in His rage,
     ⁶"But I have installed My king
     on Zion, My holy mountain!"
⁷Let me tell of the decree:
   the LORD said to me,
   b-"You are My son,
   I have fathered you this day.-b
⁸Ask it of Me,
   and I will make the nations your domain;
   your estate, the limits of the earth.
⁹You can smash them with an iron mace,
   shatter them like potter's ware."

¹⁰So now, O kings, be prudent;
   accept discipline, you rulers of the earth!
¹¹Serve the LORD in awe;
   c-tremble with fright,-c
     ¹² d-pay homage in good faith,-d
   lest He be angered, and your way be doomed
   in the mere flash of His anger.
Happy are all who take refuge in Him.

3 A psalm of David when he fled from his son Absalom.

²O LORD, my foes are so many!
Many are those who attack me;
   ³many say of me,
   "There is no deliverance for him through God."   *Selah.*ᵃ
⁴But You, O LORD, are a shield about me,
   my glory, He who holds my head high.
⁵I cry aloud to the LORD,
   and He answers me from His holy mountain.   *Selah.*
⁶I lie down and sleep and wake again,
   for the LORD sustains me.

b-b *Compare 2 Sam. 7.14, and Ps. 89.27 ff.*
c-c *Meaning of Heb. uncertain; others "rejoice with trembling."*
d-d *Meaning of Heb. uncertain.*

ᵃ *A liturgical direction of uncertain meaning.*

7I have no fear of the myriad forces
  arrayed against me on every side.

8Rise, O LORD!
Deliver me, O my God!
For You slap all my enemies in the face;b
  You break the teeth of the wicked.
9Deliverance is the LORD's;
  Your blessing be upon Your people!   Selah.

4 a-For the leader; with instrumental music.-a A psalm of David.

2Answer me when I call,
  O God, my vindicator!
You freed me from distress;
  have mercy on me and hear my prayer.
3You men, how long will my glory be mocked,
  will you love illusions,
  have recourse to frauds?   Selah.
4Know that the LORD singles out the faithful for Himself;
  the LORD hears when I call to Him.
5So tremble, and sin no more;
  ponder it on your bed, and sigh.b
6Offer sacrifices in righteousness
  and trust in the LORD.

7Many say, "O for good days!"
c-Bestow Your favor on us,-c O LORD.
8You put joy into my heart
  when their grain and wine show increase.
9Safe and sound, I lie down and sleep,
  d-for You alone, O LORD, keep me secure.-d

5 a-For the leader; on *nehiloth*.-a A psalm of David.

2Give ear to my speech, O LORD;
  consider my utterance.

---

b Lit. "cheek."
a-a Meaning of Heb. uncertain.
b Others "be still."
c-c Lit. "Lift up the light of Your countenance upon us"; cf. Num. 6.25 f.
d-d Or "for You, O LORD, keep me alone and secure."
a-a Meaning of Heb. uncertain.

3

³Heed the sound of my cry,
  my king and God,
  for I pray to You.
⁴Hear my voice, O LORD, at daybreak;
  at daybreak I plead before You, and wait.

⁵For You are not a God who desires wickedness;
  evil cannot abide with You;
  ⁶wanton men cannot endure in Your sight.
You detest all evildoers;
  ⁷You doom those who speak lies;
  murderous, deceitful men the LORD abhors.

⁸But I, through Your abundant love, enter Your house;
  I bow down in awe at Your holy temple.
⁹O LORD, ᵇ-lead me along Your righteous [path]-ᵇ
  because of my watchful foes;
  make Your way straight before me.
¹⁰For there is no sincerity on their lips;ᶜ
  their heart is [filled with] malice;
  their throat is an open grave;
  their tongue slippery.
¹¹Condemn them, O God;
  let them fall by their own devices;
  cast them out for their many crimes,
  for they defy You.
¹²But let all who take refuge in You rejoice,
  ever jubilant as You shelter them;
  and let those who love Your name exult in You.
¹³For You surely bless the righteous man, O LORD,
  encompassing him with favor like a shield.

6 ᵃ-For the leader; with instrumental music on the *sheminith*.-ᵃ A psalm
of David.

  ²O LORD, do not punish me in anger,
    do not chastise me in fury.

ᵇ-ᵇ *Or "as You are righteous, lead me."*
ᶜ *Lit. "mouth."*

ᵃ-ᵃ *Meaning of Heb. uncertain.*

³Have mercy on me, O LORD, for I languish;
   heal me, O LORD, for my bones shake with terror.
⁴My whole being is stricken with terror,
   while You, LORD—O, how long!
⁵O LORD, turn! Rescue me!
Deliver me as befits Your faithfulness.
⁶For there is no praise of You among the dead;
   in Sheol, who can acclaim You?

⁷I am weary with groaning;
   every night I drench my bed,
   I melt my couch in tears.
⁸My eyes are wasted by vexation,
   worn out because of all my foes.
⁹Away from me, all you evildoers,
   for the LORD heeds the sound of my weeping.
¹⁰The LORD heeds my plea,
   the LORD accepts my prayer.
¹¹All my enemies will be frustrated and stricken with terror;
   they will turn back in an instant, frustrated.

7 ª⁻Shiggaion of David,⁻ª which he sang to the LORD, concerning Cush, a Benjaminite.

²O LORD, my God, in You I seek refuge;
   deliver me from all my pursuers and save me,
   ³lest, like a lion, they tear me apart,
   rending in pieces, and no one save me.
⁴O LORD, my God, if I have done such things,
   if my hands bear the guilt of wrongdoing,
   ⁵if I have dealt evil to my ally,
   —ᵇ⁻I who rescued my foe without reward⁻ᵇ—
   ⁶then let the enemy pursue and overtake me;
   let him trample my life to the ground,
   and lay my body in the dust.   Selah.

ª⁻ª Meaning of Heb. uncertain.
ᵇ⁻ᵇ Meaning of Heb. uncertain; others "or stripped my foe clean."

5

⁷Rise, O LORD, in Your anger;
    assert Yourself ᶜ‑against the fury of my foes;‑ᶜ
    bestir Yourself on my behalf;
    You have ordained judgment.
⁸ ᵃ‑Let the assembly of peoples gather about You,
    with You enthroned above, on high.‑ᵃ
⁹The LORD judges the peoples;
    vindicate me, O LORD,
    for the righteousness and blamelessness that are mine.
¹⁰Let the evil of the wicked come to an end,
    but establish the righteous;
    he who probes the mind and conscienceᵈ is God the
        righteous.
¹¹ᵉ‑I look to God to shield me;‑ᵉ
    the deliverer of the upright.
¹²God vindicates the righteous;
    God ᶠ‑pronounces doom‑ᶠ each day.
¹³ᵍ‑If one does not turn back, but whets his sword,
    bends his bow and aims it,
    ¹⁴then against himself he readies deadly weapons,
    and makes his arrows sharp.‑ᵍ
¹⁵See, he hatches evil, conceives mischief,
    and gives birth to fraud.
¹⁶He has dug a pit and deepened it,
    and will fall into the trap he made.
¹⁷His mischief will recoil upon his own head;
    his lawlessness will come down upon his skull.
¹⁸I will praise the LORD for His righteousness,
    and sing a hymn to the name of the LORD Most High.

8

ᵃ‑For the leader; on the *gittith*.‑ᵃ A psalm of David.

²O LORD, our Lord,
    How majestic is Your name throughout the earth,

ᶜ‑ᶜ *Or* "in Your fury against my foes."
ᵈ *Lit.* "kidneys."
ᵉ‑ᵉ *Cf. Ibn Ezra and Kimhi; lit.* "My Shield is upon God."
ᶠ‑ᶠ *Others* "has indignation."
ᵍ‑ᵍ *Meaning of vv. 13–14 uncertain; an alternate rendering, with God as the main subject, is:*
    ¹³*If one does not turn back, He whets His sword,/bends His bow and aims it;/*¹⁴*deadly weapons*
    He prepares for him,/and makes His arrows sharp.

ᵃ‑ᵃ *Meaning of Heb. uncertain.*

ᵇ⁻You who have covered the heavens with Your splendor! ⁻ᵇ
3ᵃ⁻From the mouths of infants and sucklings
You have founded strength on account of Your foes,
to put an end to enemy and avenger.⁻ᵃ
4When I behold Your heavens, the work of Your fingers,
the moon and stars that You set in place,
5what is man that You have been mindful of him,
mortal man that You have taken note of him,
6that You have made him little less than divine,ᶜ
and adorned him with glory and majesty;
7You have made him master over Your handiwork,
laying the world at his feet,
8sheep and oxen, all of them,
and wild beasts, too;
9the birds of the heavens, the fish of the sea,
whatever travels the paths of the seas.
10O LORD, our Lord, how majestic is Your name throughout
the earth!

9 ᵃ⁻For the leader; *'almuth labben.*⁻ᵃ A psalm of David.

2I will praise You, LORD, with all my heart;
I will tell all Your wonders.
3I will rejoice and exult in You,
singing a hymn to Your name, O Most High.

4When my enemies retreat,
they stumble to their doom at Your presence.
5For You uphold my right and claim,
enthroned as righteous judge.
6You blast the nations;
You destroy the wicked;
You blot out their name forever.
7 ᵇ⁻The enemy is no more—
ruins everlasting;
You have torn down their cities;
their very names are lost.⁻ᵇ

ᵇ⁻ᵇ *Meaning of Heb. uncertain; or "You whose splendor is celebrated all over the heavens!"*
ᶜ *Or "the angels."*
ᵃ⁻ᵃ *Meaning of Heb. uncertain; some mss. and ancient versions, 'al muth labben, as though "over the death of the son."*
ᵇ⁻ᵇ *Meaning of Heb. uncertain.*

⁸But the LORD abides forever;
  He has set up His throne for judgment;
    ⁹it is He who judges the world with righteousness,
    rules the peoples with equity.
¹⁰The LORD is a haven for the oppressed,
    a haven in times of trouble.
¹¹Those who know Your name trust You,
    for You do not abandon those who turn to You, O LORD.
¹²Sing a hymn to the LORD, ᶜ‑who reigns in Zion;‑ᶜ
    declare His deeds among the peoples.
¹³ ᵈ‑For He does not ignore the cry of the afflicted;
    He who requites bloodshed is mindful of them.‑ᵈ
¹⁴Have mercy on me, O LORD;
    see my affliction at the hands of my foes,
    You who lift me from the gates of death,
      ¹⁵so that in the gates of ᵉ‑Fair Zion‑ᵉ
    I might tell all Your praise,
    I might exult in Your deliverance.
¹⁶The nations sink in the pit they have made;
    their own foot is caught in the net they have hidden.
¹⁷The LORD has made Himself known:
  He works judgment;
    the wicked man is snared by his own devices. *Higgaion*.ᵇ *Selah*.
¹⁸Let the wicked beᶠ in Sheol,
    all the nations who ignore God!
¹⁹Not always shall the needy be ignored,
    nor the hope of the afflicted forever lost.
²⁰Rise, O LORD!
  Let not men have power;
    let the nations be judged in Your presence.
²¹ᵇ‑Strike fear into them,‑ᵇ O LORD;
    let the nations know they are only men.   *Selah*.

10

Why, O LORD, do You stand aloof,
    heedless in times of trouble?
  ²The wicked in his arrogance hounds the lowly—

ᶜ‑ᶜ *Or "O You who dwell in Zion."*
ᵈ‑ᵈ *Order of Hebrew clauses inverted for clarity.*
ᵉ‑ᵉ *Lit. "the Daughter of Zion."*
ᶠ *Others "return to."*

8

ᵃ⁻may they be caught in the schemes they devise! ⁻ᵃ

³ᵇ⁻The wicked crows about his unbridled lusts;
the grasping man reviles and scorns the LORD.

⁴The wicked, arrogant as he is,
in all his scheming [thinks],⁻ᵇ
"He does not call to account;
ᶜ⁻God does not care."⁻ᶜ

⁵His ways prosper at all times;
Your judgments are far beyond him;
he snorts at all his foes.

⁶He thinks, "I shall not be shaken,
through all time never be in trouble."

⁷His mouth is full of oaths, deceit, and fraud;
mischief and evil are under his tongue.

⁸He lurks in outlying places;
from a covert he slays the innocent;
his eyes spy out the hapless.

⁹He waits in a covert like a lion in his lair;
waits to seize the lowly;
he seizes the lowly as he pulls his net shut;
¹⁰he stoops, he crouches,
ᵇ⁻and the hapless fall prey to his might.⁻ᵇ

¹¹He thinks, "God is not mindful,
He hides His face, He never looks."

¹²Rise, O LORD!
ᵈ⁻Strike at him,⁻ᵈ O God!
Do not forget the lowly.

¹³Why should the wicked man scorn God,
thinking You do not call to account?

¹⁴You do look!
You take note of mischief and vexation!
ᵇ⁻To requite is in Your power.⁻ᵇ
To You the hapless can entrust himself;
You have ever been the orphan's help.

¹⁵O break the power of the wicked and evil man,
so that when You ᵉ⁻look for⁻ᵉ his wickedness
You will find it no more.

ᵃ⁻ᵃ *Or "they (i.e., the lowly) are caught by the schemes they devised."*
ᵇ⁻ᵇ *Meaning of Heb. uncertain.*
ᶜ⁻ᶜ *Lit. "There is no God."*
ᵈ⁻ᵈ *Lit. "Lift Your hand."*
ᵉ⁻ᵉ *A play on* darash, *which in vv. 4 and 13 means "to call to account."*

16The LORD is king for ever and ever;
   the nations will perish from His land.
17You will listen to the entreaty of the lowly, O LORD,
   You will make their hearts firm;
   You will incline Your ear
     18to champion the orphan and the downtrodden,
     b-that men who are of the earth tyrannize no more.-b

11
For the leader. Of David.

In the LORD I take refuge;
   how can you say to me,
   "Take to a-the hills like a bird! -a
2For see, the wicked bend the bow,
   they set their arrow on the string
   to shoot from the shadows at the upright.
3b-When the foundations are destroyed,
   what can the righteous man do?"-b

4The LORD is in His holy palace;
   the LORD—His throne is in heaven;
   His eyes behold, His gaze searches mankind.
5The LORD seeks out the righteous man,
   but loathes the wicked one who loves injustice.
6He will rain down upon the wicked blazing coals and sulfur;
   a scorching wind shall be c-their lot.-c
7For the LORD is righteous;
   He loves righteous deeds;
   the upright shall behold His face.

12
For the leader; on the *sheminith*. A psalm of David.

2Help, O LORD!
For the faithful are no more;
   the loyal have vanished from among men.

---

a-a *Meaning of Heb. uncertain; lit. "your hill, bird!"*
b-b *Or "For the foundations are destroyed; what has the Righteous One done?"*
  Or "If the foundations are destroyed, what has the righteous man accomplished?"
c-c *Lit. "the portion of their cup."*

³Men speak lies to one another;
　　their speech is smooth;
　　they talk with duplicity.
⁴May the LORD cut off all flattering lips,
　　every tongue that speaks arrogance.
⁵They say, "By our tongues we shall prevail;
　　with lips such as ours, who can be our master?"

⁶"Because of the groans of the plundered poor and needy,
　　I will now act," says the LORD.
ᵃ"I will give help," He affirms to him.ᵃ
⁷The words of the LORD are pure words,
　　silver purged in an earthen crucible,
　　refined sevenfold.
⁸You, O LORD, will keep them,
　　guarding each ᵃfrom this ageᵃ evermore.
⁹On every side the wicked roam
　　ᵃwhen baseness is exalted among men.ᵃ

13 For the leader. A psalm of David.

²How long, O LORD; will You ignore me forever?
How long will You hide Your face from me?
³How long will I have cares on my mind,
　　grief in my heart all day?
How long will my enemy have the upper hand?
⁴Look at me, answer me, O LORD, my God!
Restore the luster to my eyes,
　　lest I sleep the sleep of death;
　　⁵lest my enemy say, "I have overcome him,"
　　my foes exult when I totter.
⁶But I trust in Your faithfulness,
　　my heart will exult in Your deliverance.
I will sing to the LORD,
　　for He has been good to me.

ᵃ⁻ᵃ *Meaning of Heb. uncertain.*

14 ªFor the leader. Of David.

The benighted man thinks,
ᵇ⁻"God does not care."⁻ᵇ
Man's deeds are corrupt and loathsome;
no one does good.
²The LORD looks down from heaven on mankind
to find a man of understanding,
a man mindful of God.
³All have turned bad,
altogether foul;
there is none who does good,
not even one.
⁴Are they so witless, all those evildoers,
who devour my people as they devour food,
and do not invoke the LORD?
⁵There they will be seized with fright,
for God is present in the circle of the righteous.
⁶You may set at naught the counsel of the lowly,
but the LORD is his refuge.

⁷O that the deliverance of Israel might come from Zion!
When the LORD restores the fortunes of His people,
Jacob will exult, Israel will rejoice.

15 A psalm of David.

LORD, who may sojourn in Your tent,
who may dwell on Your holy mountain?
²He who lives without blame,
who does what is right,
and in his heart acknowledges the truth;
³ ª⁻whose tongue is not given to evil;⁻ª
who has never done harm to his fellow,
or borne reproach for [his acts toward] his neighbor;
⁴for whom a contemptible man is abhorrent,

ª Cf. Ps. 53.
ᵇ⁻ᵇ Lit. "There is no God"; cf. Ps. 10.4.

ª⁻ª Meaning of Heb. uncertain; or "who has no slander upon his tongue."

but who honors those who fear the LORD;
who stands by his oath even to his hurt;
5who has never lent money at interest,
or accepted a bribe against the innocent.
The man who acts thus shall never be shaken.

16 A *michtam*[a] of David.

Protect me, O God, for I seek refuge in You.
2I say to the LORD,
"You are my Lord, [b-]my benefactor;
there is none above You."[-b]
3 [c-]As to the holy and mighty ones that are in the land,
my whole desire concerning them is that
4those who espouse another [god]
may have many sorrows! [-c]
I will have no part of their bloody libations;
their names will not pass my lips.
5The LORD is my allotted share and portion;[d]
You control my fate.
6Delightful country has fallen to my lot;
lovely indeed is my estate.
7I bless the LORD who has guided me;
my conscience[e] admonishes me at night.
8I am ever mindful of the LORD's presence;
He is at my right hand; I shall never be shaken.
9So my heart rejoices,
my whole being exults,
and my body rests secure.
10For You will not abandon me to Sheol,
or let Your faithful one see the Pit.
11You will teach me the path of life.
In Your presence is perfect joy;
delights are ever in Your right hand.

---

[a] *Meaning of Heb. uncertain.*
[b-b] *Others "I have no good but in You."*
[c-c] *Meaning of Heb. uncertain; "holy and mighty ones" taken as epithets for divine beings; cf.* qedoshim *in Ps. 89.6, 8, and* 'addirim *in 1 Sam. 4.8.*
[d] *Lit. "cup."*
[e] *Lit. "kidneys."*

17 A prayer of David.

Hear, O LORD, what is just;
heed my cry, give ear to my prayer,
uttered without guile.
²My vindication will come from You;
Your eyes will behold what is right.
³You have visited me at night, probed my mind,
You have tested me and found nothing amiss;
ᵃ⁻I determined that my mouth should not transgress.
⁴As for man's dealings,
in accord with the command of Your lips,⁻ᵃ
I have kept in view the fateᵇ of the lawless.
⁵My feet have held to Your paths;
my legs have not given way.

⁶I call on You;
You will answer me, God;
turn Your ear to me,
hear what I say.
⁷Display Your faithfulness in wondrous deeds,
You who deliver with Your right hand
those who seek refuge from assailants.
⁸Guard me like the apple of Your eye;
hide me in the shadow of Your wings
⁹from the wicked who despoil me,
ᶜ⁻my mortal enemies who⁻ᶜ encircle me.
¹⁰ ᵃ⁻Their hearts are closed to pity;⁻ᵃ
they mouth arrogance;
¹¹now they hem in our feet on every side;
they set their eyes roaming over the land.
¹²He is like a lion eager for prey,
a king of beasts lying in wait.

¹³Rise, O LORD! Go forth to meet him.
Bring him down;
rescue me from the wicked with Your sword,

ᵃ⁻ᵃ *Meaning of Heb. uncertain.*
ᵇ *Cf. Prov. 1.19; lit. "paths."*
ᶜ⁻ᶜ *Or "from my enemies who avidly."*

14 a-from men, O LORD, with Your hand,
  from men whose share in life is fleeting.
But as to Your treasured ones,
  fill their bellies. -a
Their sons too shall be satisfied,
  and have something to leave over for their young.
15Then I, justified, will behold Your face;
  awake, I am filled with the vision of You.

18

aFor the leader. Of David, the servant of the LORD, who addressed the words of this song to the LORD after the LORD had saved him from the hands of all his enemies and from the clutches of Saul.

2He said:
  b-I adore you, O LORD, my strength,-b
  3O LORD, my crag, my fortress, my rescuer,
  my God, my rock in whom I seek refuge,
  my shield, my c-mighty champion,-c my haven.
4 d-All praise! I called on the LORD-d
  and was delivered from my enemies.
5Ropese of Death encompassed me;
  torrents of Belialf terrified me;
6ropes of Sheol encircled me;
  snares of Death confronted me.
7In my distress I called on the LORD,
  cried out to my God;
  in His temple He heard my voice;
  my cry to Him reached His ears.
8Then the earth rocked and quaked;
  the foundations of the mountains shook,
  rocked by His indignation;
  9smoke went up from His nostrils,
  from His mouth came devouring fire;
  live coals blazed forth from Him.
10He bent the sky and came down,
  thick cloud beneath His feet.
11He mounted a cherub and flew,
  gliding on the wings of the wind.

a This poem occurs again at 2 Sam. 22, with a number of variations, some of which are cited in
  the following notes.
b-b Not in 2 Sam. 22.2.
c-c Lit. "horn of rescue."
d-d Construction of Heb. uncertain.
e 2 Sam. 22.5, "breakers."
f I.e., the netherworld, like "Death" and "Sheol."

¹²He made darkness His screen;
 dark thunderheads, dense clouds of the sky
 were His pavilion round about Him.
¹³Out of the brilliance before Him,
 hail and fiery coals ᵍ‑pierced His clouds.‑ᵍ
¹⁴Then the LORD thundered from heaven,
 the Most High gave forth His voice—
 ʰ‑hail and fiery coals.‑ʰ
¹⁵He let fly His shafts and scattered them;
 He discharged lightning and routed them.
¹⁶The ocean bed was exposed;
 the foundations of the world were laid bare
 by Your mighty roaring, O LORD,
 at the blast of the breath of Your nostrils.
¹⁷He reached down from on high, He took me;
 He drew me out of the mighty waters;
¹⁸He saved me from my fierce enemy,
 from foes too strong for me.
¹⁹They confronted me on the day of my calamity,
 but the LORD was my support.
²⁰He brought me out to freedom;
 He rescued me because He was pleased with me.

²¹The LORD rewarded me according to my merit;
 He requited the cleanness of my hands;
 ²²for I have kept to the ways of the LORD,
 and have not been guilty before my God;
 ²³for I am mindful of all His rules;
 I have not disregarded His laws.
²⁴I have been blameless toward Him,
 and have guarded myself against sinning;
 ²⁵and the LORD has requited me according to my merit,
 the cleanness of my hands in His sight.

²⁶With the loyal, You deal loyally;
 with the blameless man, blamelessly.
²⁷With the pure, You act purely,
 and with the perverse, You are wily.
²⁸It is You who deliver lowly folk,

ᵍ⁻ᵍ *2 Sam. 22.13, "blazed."*
ʰ⁻ʰ *Not in 2 Sam. 22.14.*

but haughty eyes You humble.
29It is You who light my lamp;
  the LORD, my God, lights up my darkness.
30With You, I can rush a barrier;[i]
  with my God I can scale a wall;
    31the way of God is perfect;
    the word of the LORD is pure;
    He is a shield to all who seek refuge in Him.
32Truly, who is a god except the LORD,
  who is a rock but our God?—
    33the God who girded me with might,
    who made my way perfect;
    34who made my legs like a deer's,
    and let me stand firm on the[j] heights;
    35who trained my hands for battle;
    my arms can bend a bow of bronze.
36You have given me the shield of Your protection;
  Your right hand has sustained me,
  Your care[k] has made me great.
37You have let me stride on freely;
  my feet have not slipped.
38I pursued my enemies and overtook them;
  I did not turn back till I destroyed them.
39I struck them down,
  and they could rise no more;
  they lay fallen at my feet.
40You have girded me with strength for battle,
  brought my adversaries low before me,
    41made my enemies turn tail before me;
    I wiped out my foes.
42They cried out, but there was none to deliver;
  [cried] to the LORD, but He did not answer them.
43I ground them fine as windswept dust;
  I trod them flat as dirt of the streets.
44You have rescued me from the strife of people;
  You have set me at the head of nations;
  peoples I knew not must serve me.
45At the mere report of me they are submissive;

---

i Cf. note to 2 Sam. 22.30; or "troop."
j Taking bamothai as a poetic form of bamoth; cf. Hab. 3.19; others "my."
k Meaning of Heb. uncertain; others "condescension."

foreign peoples cower before me;
⁴⁶foreign peoples lose courage,
ⁱ·and come trembling out of their strongholds.·ⁱ

⁴⁷The LORD lives! Blessed is my rock!
Exalted be God, my deliverer,
⁴⁸the God who has vindicated me
and made peoples subject to me,
⁴⁹who rescued me from my enemies,
who raised me clear of my adversaries,
saved me from lawless men.
⁵⁰For this I sing Your praise among the nations, LORD,
and hymn Your name:
⁵¹ᵐ·He accords great victories·ᵐ to His king,
keeps faith with His anointed,
with David and his offspring forever.

19

For the leader. A psalm of David.

²The heavens declare the glory of God,
the sky proclaims His handiwork.
³Day to day makes utterance,
night to night speaks out.
⁴There is no utterance,
there are no words,
ᵃ·whose sound goes unheard.·ᵃ
⁵Their voiceᵇ carries throughout the earth,
their words to the end of the world.
He placed in themᶜ a tent for the sun,
⁶who is like a groom coming forth from the chamber,
like a hero, eager to run his course.
⁷His rising-place is at one end of heaven,
and his circuit reaches the other;
nothing escapes his heat.

⁸The teaching of the LORD is perfect,
renewing life;

ⁱ·ⁱ *Meaning of Heb. uncertain.*
ᵐ·ᵐ *2 Sam. 22.51, "Tower of victory."*

ᵃ·ᵃ *With Septuagint, Symmachus, and Vulgate; or "their sound is not heard."*
ᵇ *Cf. Septuagint, Symmachus, and Vulgate; Arabic* qawwah, *"to shout."*
ᶜ *Viz., the heavens.*

the decrees of the LORD are enduring,
making the simple wise;
9The precepts of the LORD are just,
rejoicing the heart;
the instruction of the LORD is lucid,
making the eyes light up.
10The fear of the LORD is pure,
abiding forever;
the judgments of the LORD are true,
righteous altogether,
11more desirable than gold,
than much fine gold;
sweeter than honey,
than drippings of the comb.
12Your servant pays them heed;
in obeying them there is much reward.
13Who can be aware of errors?
Clear me of unperceived guilt,
14and from d-willful sins-d keep Your servant;
let them not dominate me;
then shall I be blameless
and clear of grave offense.
15May the words of my mouth
and the prayer of my hearte
be acceptable to You,
O LORD, my rock and my redeemer.

20 For the leader. A psalm of David.

2May the LORD answer you in time of trouble,
the name of Jacob's God keep you safe.
3May He send you help from the sanctuary,
and sustain you from Zion.
4May He receive the tokensa of all your meal offerings,
and approveb your burnt offerings.   *Selah*.
5May He grant you your desire,
and fulfill your every plan.

---

d-d Or "arrogant men"; cf. Ps. 119.51.
e For leb as a source of speech, see note to Eccl. 5.1.

a Reference to azkara, "token portion" of meal offering; Lev. 2.2, 9, 16, etc.
b Meaning of Heb. uncertain.

⁶May we shout for joy in your victory,
    arrayed by standards in the name of our God.
May the LORD fulfill your every wish.

⁷Now I know that the LORD will give victory to His anointed,
    will answer him from His heavenly sanctuary
    with the mighty victories of His right arm.
⁸They [call] on chariots, they [call] on horses,
    but we call on the name of the LORD our God.
⁹They collapse and lie fallen,
    but we rally and gather strength.
¹⁰ᶜ-O LORD, grant victory!
May the King answer us when we call.-ᶜ

21 For the leader. A psalm of David.

²O LORD, the king rejoices in Your strength;
    how greatly he exults in Your victory!
³You have granted him the desire of his heart,
    have not denied the request of his lips.   Selah.
⁴You have proffered him blessings of good things,
    have set upon his head a crown of fine gold.
⁵He asked You for life; You granted it;
    a long life, everlasting.
⁶Great is his glory through Your victory;
    You have endowed him with splendor and majesty.
⁷You have made him blessed forever,
    gladdened him with the joy of Your presence.
⁸For the king trusts in the LORD;
    Through the faithfulness of the Most High
    he will not be shaken.
⁹Your hand is equal to all Your enemies;
    Your right hand overpowers Your foes.
¹⁰You set them ablaze like a furnace
    ᵃ-when You show Your presence.-ᵃ
The LORD in anger destroys them;

ᶜ-ᶜ Or, in the light of v. 7, "O LORD, grant victory to the king; may He answer us when we call."
ᵃ-ᵃ Or "at the time of Your anger."

20

fire consumes them.
11You wipe their offspring from the earth,
their issue from among men.
12For they schemed against You;
they laid plans,
but could not succeed.
13b-For You make them turn back-b
by Your bows aimed at their face.
14Be exalted, O LORD, through Your strength;
we will sing and chant the praises of Your mighty deeds.

22 For the leader; on a-ayyeleth ha-shahar.-a A psalm of David.

2My God, my God,
why have You abandoned me;
why so far from delivering me
and from my anguished roaring?
3My God,
I cry by day—You answer not;
by night, and have no respite.

4b-But You are the Holy One,
enthroned,
the Praise of Israel.-b
5In You our fathers trusted;
they trusted, and You rescued them.
6To You they cried out
and they escaped;
in You they trusted
and were not disappointed.

7But I am a worm, less than human;
scorned by men, despised by people.
8All who see me mock me;
c-they curl their lips,-c
they shake their heads.

b-b *Meaning of Heb. uncertain.*

a-a *Meaning of Heb. uncertain.*
b-b *Or "But You are holy, enthroned upon the praises of Israel."*
c-c *Lit. "they open wide with a lip."*

9"Let him commit himself to the LORD;
  let Him rescue him,
  let Him save him,
  for He is pleased with him."
10You a-drew me-a from the womb,
  made me secure at my mother's breast.
11I became Your charge at birth;
  from my mother's womb You have been my God.
12Do not be far from me,
  for trouble is near,
  and there is none to help.
13Many bulls surround me,
  mighty ones of Bashan encircle me.
14They open their mouths at me
  like tearing, roaring lions.
15d-My life ebbs away:-d
  all my bones are disjointed;
  my heart is like wax,
  melting within me;
  16my vigor dries up like a shard;
  my tongue cleaves to my palate;
  You commit me to the dust of death.
17Dogs surround me;
  a pack of evil ones closes in on me,
  e-like lions [they maul] my hands and feet.-e
18I take the count of all my bones
  while they look on and gloat.
19They divide my clothes among themselves,
  casting lots for my garments.

20But You, O LORD, be not far off;
  my strength, hasten to my aid.
21Save my life from the sword,
  my precious lifef from the clutches of a dog.
22Deliver me from a lion's mouth;
  from the horns of wild oxen rescueg me.
23Then will I proclaim Your fame to my brethren,
  praise You in the congregation.

d-d Lit. "I am poured out like water."
e-e With Rashi; cf. Isa. 38.13.
f Lit. "only one."
g Lit. "answer."

22

24You who fear the LORD, praise Him!
All you offspring of Jacob, honor Him!
Be in dread of Him, all you offspring of Israel!
25For He did not scorn, He did not spurn
    the plea[h] of the lowly;
    He did not hide His face from him;
    when he cried out to Him, He listened.
26 i-Because of You I offer praise-i in the great congregation;
    I pay my vows in the presence of His worshipers.
27Let the lowly eat and be satisfied;
    let all who seek the LORD praise Him.
Always be of good cheer!
28Let all the ends of the earth pay heed and turn to the LORD,
    and the peoples of all nations prostrate themselves before
        You;
    29for kingship is the LORD's
    and He rules the nations.
30j-All those in full vigor shall eat and prostrate themselves;
    all those at death's door, whose spirits flag,
    shall bend the knee before Him.-j
31Offspring shall serve Him;
    the LORD's fame shall be proclaimed to the generation
    32to come;
    they shall tell of His beneficence
    to people yet to be born,
    for He has acted.

23 A psalm of David.

The LORD is my shepherd;
    I lack nothing.
2He makes me lie down in green pastures;
    He leads me to a-water in places of repose;-a
    3He renews my life;
    He guides me in right paths
    as befits His name.

h Or "plight."
i-i Lit. "From You is my praise."
j-j Meaning of Heb. uncertain; others "All the fat ones of the earth shall eat and worship;/All
    they that go down to the dust shall kneel before Him,/Even he that cannot keep his soul alive."

a-a Others "still waters."

⁴Though I walk through ᵇ⁻a valley of deepest darkness,⁻ᵇ
    I fear no harm, for You are with me;
    Your rod and Your staff—they comfort me.

⁵You spread a table for me in full view of my enemies;
    You anoint my head with oil;
    my drink is abundant.
⁶Only goodness and steadfast love shall pursue me
    all the days of my life,
    and I shall dwell in the house of the LORD
    for many long years.

24 Of David. A psalm.

The earth is the LORD's and all that it holds,
    the world and its inhabitants.
²For He founded it upon the ocean,
    set it on the nether-streams.

³Who may ascend the mountain of the LORD?
Who may stand in His holy place?—
⁴He who has clean hands and a pure heart,
    who has not taken a false oath by Myᵃ life
    or sworn deceitfully.
⁵He shall carry away a blessing from the LORD,
    a just reward from God, his deliverer.
⁶Such is the circleᵇ of those who turn to Him,
    Jacob, who seek Your presence.   Selah.

⁷O gates, lift up your heads!
Up high, you everlasting doors,
    so the King of glory may come in!
⁸Who is the King of glory?—
    the LORD, mighty and valiant,
    the LORD, valiant in battle.
⁹O gates, lift up your heads!
Lift them up, you everlasting doors,
    so the King of glory may come in!

ᵇ⁻ᵇ *Others "the valley of the shadow of death."*

ᵃ *Ancient versions and some mss. read "His."*
ᵇ *Lit. "generation."*

¹⁰Who is the King of glory?—
  the LORD of hosts,
  He is the King of glory!   *Selah.*

25 Of David.

א   O LORD, I set my hope on You;
ב   ²my God, in You I trust;
        may I not be disappointed,
        may my enemies not exult over me.
ג   ³O let none who look to You be disappointed;
        let the faithless be disappointed, empty-handed.
ד   ⁴Let me know Your paths, O LORD;
        teach me Your ways;
הו   ⁵guide me in Your true way and teach me,
        for You are God, my deliverer;
        it is You I look to at all times.
ז   ⁶O LORD, be mindful of Your compassion
        and Your faithfulness;
        they are old as time.
ח   ⁷Be not mindful of my youthful sins and transgressions;
        in keeping with Your faithfulness consider what is in my
           favor,
        as befits Your goodness, O LORD.
ט   ⁸Good and upright is the LORD;
        therefore He shows sinners the way.
י   ⁹He guides the lowly in the right path,
        and teaches the lowly His way.
כ   ¹⁰All the LORD'S paths are steadfast love
        for those who keep the decrees of His covenant.
ל   ¹¹As befits Your name, O LORD,
        pardon my iniquity though it be great.
מ   ¹²Whoever fears the LORD,
        he shall be shown what path to choose.
נ   ¹³He shall live a happy life,
        and his children shall inherit the land.
ס   ¹⁴The counsel[a] of the LORD is for those who fear Him;

ᵃ Or *"secret."*

to them He makes known His covenant.

ע   15My eyes are ever toward the LORD,
       for He will loose my feet from the net.

פ   16Turn to me, have mercy on me,
       for I am alone and afflicted.

צ   17b-My deep distress-b increases;
       deliver me from my straits.

ר   18Look at my affliction and suffering,
       and forgive all my sins.
       19See how numerous my enemies are,
       and how unjustly they hate me!

ש   20Protect me and save me;
       let me not be disappointed,
       for I have sought refuge in You.

ת   21May integrity and uprightness watch over me,
       for I look to You.
       22O God, redeem Israel
       from all its distress.

26 Of David.

Vindicate me, O LORD,
    for I have walked without blame;
    I have trusted in the LORD;
    I have not faltered.
    2Probe me, O LORD, and try me,
       test my a-heart and mind;-a
       3 b-for my eyes are on Your steadfast love;
       I have set my course by it.-b
    4I do not consort with scoundrels,
       or mix with hypocrites;
    5I detest the company of evil men,
       and do not consort with the wicked;
    6I wash my hands in innocence,
       and walk around Your altar, O LORD,
    7raising my voice in thanksgiving,
       and telling all Your wonders.

---

b-b Lit. "The distress of my heart."

a-a Lit. "kidneys and heart."
b-b Or "I am aware of Your faithfulness, and always walk in Your true [path]."

8O LORD, I love Your temple abode,
the dwelling-place of Your glory.
9Do not sweep me away with sinners,
or [snuff out] my life with murderers,
10who have schemes at their fingertips,
and hands full of bribes.
11But I walk without blame;
redeem me, have mercy on me!
12My feet are on level ground.
In assemblies I will bless the LORD.

27 Of David.

The LORD is my light and my help;
whom should I fear?
The LORD is the stronghold of my life,
whom should I dread?
2When evil men assail me
a-to devour my flesh-a—
it is they, my foes and my enemies,
who stumble and fall.
3Should an army besiege me,
my heart would have no fear;
should war beset me,
still would I be confident.

4One thing I ask of the LORD,
only that do I seek:
to live in the house of the LORD
all the days of my life,
to gaze upon the beauty of the LORD,
b-to frequent-b His temple.
5He will shelter me in His pavilion
on an evil day,
grant me the protection of His tent,
raise me high upon a rock.
6Now is my head high

a-a Or "to slander me"; cf. Dan. 3.8; 6.25.
b-b Meaning of Heb. uncertain.

27

over my enemies roundabout;
I sacrifice in His tent with shouts of joy,
singing and chanting a hymn to the LORD.

7Hear, O LORD, when I cry aloud;
have mercy on me, answer me.
8 b-In Your behalf-b my heart says:
"Seek My face!"
O LORD, I seek Your face.
9Do not hide Your face from me;
do not thrust aside Your servant in anger;
You have ever been my help.
Do not forsake me, do not abandon me,
O God, my deliverer.
10Though my father and mother abandon me,
the LORD will take me in.
11Show me Your way, O LORD,
and lead me on a level path
because of my watchful foes.
12Do not subject me to the will of my foes,
for false witnesses and unjust accusers
have appeared against me.
13Had I not the assurance
that I would enjoy the goodness of the LORD
in the land of the living . . .

14Look to the LORD;
be strong and of good courage!
O look to the LORD!

28 Of David.

O LORD, I call to You;
my rock, do not disregard me,
for if You hold aloof from me,
I shall be like those gone down into the Pit.
2Listen to my plea for mercy

  when I cry out to You,
  when I lift my hands
   toward Your inner sanctuary.
³Do not ᵃ‑count me‑ᵃ with the wicked and evildoers
  who profess goodwill toward their fellows
   while malice is in their heart.
⁴Pay them according to their deeds,
  their malicious acts;
  according to their handiwork pay them,
   give them their deserts.
⁵For they do not consider the LORD's deeds,
  the work of His hands.
May He tear them down,
  never to rebuild them!
⁶Blessed is the LORD,
  for He listens to my plea for mercy.
⁷The LORD is my strength and my shield;
  my heart trusts in Him.
I was helped,ᵇ and my heart exulted,
  so I will glorify Him with my song.
⁸The LORD is ᶜ‑their strength;‑ᶜ
  He is a stronghold for the deliverance of His anointed.
⁹Deliver and bless Your very own people;
  tend them and sustain them forever.

29 A psalm of David.

  Ascribe to the LORD, O divine beings,
   ascribe to the LORD glory and strength.
²Ascribe to the LORD the glory of His name;
  bow down to the LORD, majestic in holiness.
³The voice of the LORD is over the waters;
  the God of glory thunders,
   the LORD, over the mighty waters.
⁴The voice of the LORD is power;
  the voice of the LORD is majesty;
   ⁵the voice of the LORD breaks cedars;

ᵃ‑ᵃ Or "drag me off"; meaning of Heb. uncertain.
ᵇ Or "strengthened."
ᶜ‑ᶜ Septuagint, Saadia, and others render, and some mss. read, 'oz le'ammo, "the strength of His people."

the LORD shatters the cedars of Lebanon.
6a⋅He makes Lebanon skip like a calf,⋅a
  Sirion, like a young wild ox.
7The voice of the LORD kindles flames of fire;
  8the voice of the LORD convulses the wilderness;
  the LORD convulses the wilderness of Kadesh;
  9the voice of the LORD causes hinds to calve,
  b⋅and strips forests bare;⋅b
  while in His temple all say "Glory!"
10The LORD sat enthroned at the Flood;
  the LORD sits enthroned, king forever.

11May the LORD grant strength to His people;
  may the LORD bestow on His people wellbeing.

30 A psalm of David. A song for the dedication of the House.a

2I extol You, O LORD,
  for You have lifted me up,
  and not let my enemies rejoice over me.
3O LORD, my God,
  I cried out to You,
  and You healed me.
4O LORD, You brought me up from Sheol,
  preserved me from going down into the Pit.

5O you faithful of the LORD, sing to Him,
  and praise His holy name.
6For He is angry but a moment,
  and when He is pleased there is life.
b⋅One may lie down weeping at nightfall;⋅b
  but at dawn there are shouts of joy.

7When I was untroubled,
  I thought, "I shall never be shaken,"
8for you, O LORD, when You were pleased,

---

a-a *Lit. "He makes them skip like a calf, Lebanon and Sirion, etc."*
b-b *Or "brings ewes to early birth."*

a *I.e., the Temple.*
b-b *Or "Weeping may linger for the night."*

made [me]c firm as a mighty mountain.
When You hid Your face,
    I was terrified.
9I called to You, O LORD;
    to my LORD I made appeal,
      10"What is to be gained from my death,d
      from my descent into the Pit?
Can dust praise You?
Can it declare Your faithfulness?
11Hear, O LORD, and have mercy on me;
    O LORD, be my help!"

12You turned my lament into dancing,
    you undid my sackcloth and girded me with joy,
      13that [my] whole being might sing hymns to You endlessly;
    O LORD my God, I will praise You forever.

31 For the leader. A psalm of David.

2I seek refuge in You, O LORD;
    may I never be disappointed;
    as You are righteous, rescue me.
3Incline Your ear to me;
    be quick to save me;
    be a rock, a stronghold for me,
    a citadel, for my deliverance.
4For You are my rock and my fortress;
    You lead me and guide me as befits Your name.
5You free me from the net laid for me,
    for You are my stronghold.
6Into Your hand I entrust my spirit;
    You redeem me, O LORD, faithful God.
7I detest those who rely on empty folly,
    but I trust in the LORD.
8Let me exult and rejoice in Your faithfulness
    when You notice my affliction,

c Following Saadia, R. Isaiah of Trani; cf. Ibn Ezra.
d Lit. "blood."

are mindful of my deep distress,
⁹and do not hand me over to my enemy,
but ᵃ⁻grant me relief.⁻ᵃ

¹⁰Have mercy on me, O LORD,
for I am in distress;
my eyes are wasted by vexation,
ᵇ⁻my substance and body too.⁻ᵇ
¹¹My life is spent in sorrow,
my years in groaning;
my strength fails because of my iniquity,
my limbs waste away.
¹²Because of all my foes
I am the particular butt of my neighbors,
a horror to my friends;
those who see me on the street avoid me.
¹³I am put out of mind like the dead;
I am like an object given up for lost.
¹⁴I hear the whisperings of many,
intrigueᶜ on every side,
as they scheme together against me,
plotting to take my life.

¹⁵But I trust in You, O LORD;
I say, "You are my God!"
¹⁶My fate is in Your hand;
save me from the hand of my enemies and pursuers.
¹⁷Show favor to Your servant;
as You are faithful, deliver me.
¹⁸O LORD, let me not be disappointed when I call You;
let the wicked be disappointed;
let them be silenced in Sheol;
¹⁹let lying lips be stilled
that speak haughtily against the righteous
with arrogance and contempt.
²⁰How abundant is the good
that You have in store for those who fear You,
that You do in the full view of men

ᵃ⁻ᵃ Lit. "make my feet stand in a broad place."
ᵇ⁻ᵇ Meaning of Heb. uncertain.
ᶜ Others "terror."

for those who take refuge in You.
²¹You grant them the protection of Your presence
ᵇ⁻against scheming men;⁻ᵇ
You shelter them in Your pavilion
from contentious tongues.
²²Blessed is the LORD,
for He has been wondrously faithful to me,
a veritable bastion.
²³Alarmed, I had thought,
"I am thrust out of Your sight";
yet You listened to my plea for mercy
when I cried out to You.
²⁴So love the LORD, all you faithful;
the LORD guards the loyal,
and more than requites
him who acts arrogantly.
²⁵Be strong and of good courage,
all you who wait for the LORD.

32 Of David. ᵃ⁻A *maskil.*⁻ᵃ

Happy is he whose transgression is forgiven,
whose sin is covered over.
²Happy the man whom the LORD does not hold guilty,
and in whose spirit there is no deceit.

³As long as I said nothing,
my limbs wasted away
from my anguished roaring all day long.
⁴For night and day
Your hand lay heavy on me;
my vigor waned
as in the summer drought.   *Selah.*
⁵Then I acknowledged my sin to You;
I did not cover up my guilt;
I resolved, "I will confess my transgressions to the LORD,"
and You forgave the guilt of my sin.   *Selah.*

ᵃ⁻ᵃ *Meaning of Heb. uncertain.*

33

⁶Therefore let every faithful man pray to You
ᵇ⁻upon discovering [his sin],⁻ᵇ
that the rushing mighty waters
not overtake him.
⁷You are my shelter;
You preserve me from distress;
You surround me with the joyous shouts of deliverance.

Selah.

⁸Let me enlighten you
and show you which way to go;
let me offer counsel; my eye is on you.
⁹Be not like a senseless horse or mule
ᵃ⁻whose movement must be curbed by bit and bridle;⁻ᵃ
ᶜ⁻far be it from you!⁻ᶜ
¹⁰Many are the torments of the wicked,
but he who trusts in the LORD
shall be surrounded with favor.
¹¹Rejoice in the LORD and exult, O you righteous;
shout for joy, all upright men!

33 Sing forth, O you righteous, to the LORD;
it is fit that the upright acclaim Him.
²Praise the LORD with the lyre;
with the ten-stringed harp sing to Him;
³sing Him a new song;
play sweetly with shouts of joy.
⁴For the word of the LORD is right;
His every deed is faithful.
⁵He loves what is right and just;
the earth is full of the LORD's faithful care.
⁶By the word of the LORD the heavens were made,
by the breath of His mouth, all their host.
⁷He heaps up the ocean waters like a mound,
stores the deep in vaults.

⁸Let all the earth fear the LORD;
let all the inhabitants of the world dread Him.

ᵇ⁻ᵇ *Meaning of Heb. uncertain; others "in a time when You may be found."*
ᶜ⁻ᶜ *Meaning of Heb. uncertain; for this rendering cf. Ibn Ezra.*

9For He spoke, and it was;
　He commanded, and it endured.
10The LORD frustrates the plans of nations,
　brings to naught the designs of peoples.
11What the LORD plans endures forever,
　what He designs, for ages on end.

12Happy the nation whose God is the LORD,
　the people He has chosen to be His own.
13The LORD looks down from heaven;
　He sees all mankind.
14From His dwelling-place He gazes
　on all the inhabitants of the earth—
15He who fashions the hearts of them all,
　who discerns all their doings.

16Kings are not delivered by a large force;
　warriors are not saved by great strength;
17horses are a false hope for deliverance;
　for all their great power they provide no escape.
18Truly the eye of the LORD is on those who fear Him,
　who wait for His faithful care
19to save them from death,
　to sustain them in famine.
20We set our hope on the LORD,
　He is our help and shield;
21in Him our hearts rejoice,
　for in His holy name we trust.
22May we enjoy, O LORD, Your faithful care,
　as we have put our hope in You.

34 Of David, a-when he feigned madness in the presence of Abimelech, who turned him out, and he left.-a

א　2I bless the LORD at all times;
　　praise of Him is ever in my mouth.
ב　3I glory in the LORD;

a-a Cf. 1 Sam. 21.14 ff.

let the lowly hear it and rejoice.

ג   4Exalt the LORD with me;
    let us extol His name together.

ד   5I turned to the LORD, and He answered me;
    He saved me from all my terrors.

ה   6Men look to Him and are radiant;
ו   let their faces not be downcast.

ז   7Here was a lowly man who called,
    and the LORD listened,
    and delivered him from all his troubles.

ח   8The angel of the LORD camps around those who fear Him
    and rescues them.

ט   9Taste and see how good the LORD is;
    happy the man who takes refuge in Him!

י   10Fear the LORD, you His consecrated ones,
    for those who fear Him lack nothing.

כ   11Lions have been reduced to starvation,
    but those who turn to the LORD shall not lack any good.

ל   12Come, my sons, listen to me;
    I will teach you what it is to fear the LORD.

מ   13Who is the man who is eager for life,
    who desires years of good fortune?

נ   14Guard your tongue from evil,
    your lips from deceitful speech.

ס   15Shun evil and do good,
    seek amityb and pursue it.

ע   16The eyes of the LORD are on the righteous,
    His ears attentive to their cry.

פ   17The face of the LORD is set against evildoers,
    to erase their names from the earth.

צ   18Theyc cry out, and the LORD hears,
    and saves them from all their troubles.

ק   19The LORD is close to the brokenhearted;
    those crushed in spirit He delivers.

ר   20Though the misfortunes of the righteous be many,
    the LORD will save him from them all,

ש   21Keeping all his bones intact,
    not one of them being broken.

b Or *"integrity."*
c Viz., *the righteous of v. 16.*

ח   22One misfortune is the deathblow of the wicked;
      the foes of the righteous shall be ruined.
    23The LORD redeems the life of His servants;
      all who take refuge in Him shall not be ruined.

35 Of David.

O LORD, strive with my adversaries,
    give battle to my foes,
  2take up shield and buckler,
    and come to my defense;
  3ready the spear and javelin
    against my pursuers;
    tell me, "I am your deliverance."
  4Let those who seek my life
    be frustrated and put to shame;
    let those who plan to harm me
    fall back in disgrace.
  5Let them be as chaff in the wind,
    the LORD's angel driving them on.
  6Let their path be dark and slippery,
    with the LORD's angel in pursuit.
  7For without cause they hid a net to trap me;
    without cause they dug a pit[a] for me.
  8Let disaster overtake them unawares;
    let the net they hid catch them;
    let them fall into it when disaster [strikes].
  9Then shall I exult in the LORD,
    rejoice in His deliverance.
  10All my bones shall say,
    "LORD, who is like You?
You save the poor from one stronger than he,
    the poor and needy from his despoiler."

  11Malicious witnesses appear
    who question me about things I do not know.
  12They repay me evil for good,

---

a Transferred from first clause for clarity.

[seeking] my bereavement.

13Yet, when they were ill,
  my dress was sackcloth,
  I kept a fast—
  b-may what I prayed for happen to me!-b
14I walked about as though it were my friend or my brother;
  I was bowed with gloom, like one mourning for his mother.
15But when I stumble, they gleefully gather;
  wretches gather against me,
  I know not why;
  c-they tear at me without end.
16With impious, mocking grimace-c
  they gnash their teeth at me.

17O Lord, how long will You look on?
Rescue me c-from their attacks,-c
  my precious life, from the lions,
18that I may praise You in a great congregation,
  acclaim You in a mighty throng.
19Let not my treacherous enemies rejoice over me,
  or those who hate me without reason wink their eyes.
20For they do not offer amity,
  but devise fraudulent schemes against harmless folk.
21They open wide their mouths at me,
  saying, "Aha, aha, we have seen it!"

22You have seen it, O LORD;
  do not hold aloof!
O Lord, be not far from me!
23Wake, rouse Yourself for my cause,
  for my claim, O my God and my Lord!
24Take up my cause, O LORD my God, as You are beneficent,
  and let them not rejoice over me.
25Let them not think,
  "Aha, just what we wished!"
Let them not say,
  "We have destroyed him!"
26May those who rejoice at my misfortune

---

b-b Meaning of Heb. uncertain; lit. "my prayer returns upon my bosom."
c-c Meaning of Heb. uncertain.

be frustrated and utterly disgraced;
may those who vaunt themselves over me
be clad in frustration and shame.
²⁷May those who desire my vindication
sing forth joyously;
may they always say,
"Extolled be the LORD
who desires the well-being of His servant,"
²⁸while my tongue shall recite Your beneficent acts,
Your praises all day long.

36 For the leader. Of the servant of the LORD, of David.

^{2a-}I know^{-a} what Transgression says to the wicked;
he has no sense of the dread of God,
^{3b-}because its speech is seductive to him
till his iniquity be found out and he be hated.^{-b}
⁴His words are evil and deceitful;
he will not consider doing good.
⁵In bed he plots mischief;
he is set on a path of no good,
he does not reject evil.

⁶O LORD, Your faithfulness reaches to heaven;
Your steadfastness to the sky;
⁷Your beneficence is like the high mountains;
Your justice like the great deep;
man and beast You deliver, O LORD.
⁸How precious is Your faithful care, O God!
Mankind shelters in the shadow of Your wings.
⁹They feast on the rich fare of Your house;
You let them drink at Your refreshing stream.
¹⁰With You is the fountain of life;
by Your light do we see light.
¹¹Bestow Your faithful care on those devoted to You,
and Your beneficence on upright men.
¹²Let not the foot of the arrogant tread on me,
or the hand of the wicked drive me away.

a-a *Lit. "In my heart is."*
b-b *Meaning of Heb. uncertain.*

¹³There lie the evildoers, fallen,
thrust down, unable to rise.

37 Of David.

א   Do not be vexed by evil men;
do not be incensed by wrongdoers;
²for they soon wither like grass,
like verdure fade away.

ב   ³Trust in the LORD and do good,
abide in the land and remain loyal.
⁴Seek the favor of the LORD,
and He will grant you the desires of your heart.

ג   ⁵Leave allᵃ to the LORD;
trust in Him; He will do it.
⁶He will cause your vindication to shine forth like the light,
the justice of your case, like the noonday sun.

ד   ⁷Be patient and wait for the LORD,
do not be vexed by the prospering man
who carries out his schemes.

ה   ⁸Give up anger, abandon fury,
do not be vexed;
it can only do harm.
⁹For evil men will be cut off,
but those who look to the LORD—
they shall inherit the land.

ו   ¹⁰A little longer and there will be no wicked man;
you will look at where he was—
he will be gone.
¹¹But the lowly shall inherit the land,
and delight in abundant well-being.

ז   ¹²The wicked man schemes against the righteous,
and gnashes his teeth at him.
¹³The Lord laughs at him,
for He knows that his day will come.

ח   ¹⁴The wicked draw their swords, bend their bows,

ᵃ Lit. "your way."

40

to bring down the lowly and needy,
to slaughter ᵇ-upright men.-ᵇ

¹⁵Their swords shall pierce their own hearts,
and their bows shall be broken.

ט ¹⁶Better the little that the righteous man has
than the great abundance of the wicked.

¹⁷For the arms of the wicked shall be broken,
but the LORD is the support of the righteous.

י ¹⁸The LORD is concerned for the needsᶜ of the blameless;
their portion lasts forever;
¹⁹they shall not come to grief in bad times;
in famine, they shall eat their fill.

כ ²⁰But the wicked shall perish,
and the enemies of the LORD shall be consumed,
like meadow grassᵈ consumed in smoke.

ל ²¹The wicked man borrows and does not repay;
the righteous is generous and keeps giving.

²²Those blessed by Him shall inherit the land,
but those cursed by Him shall be cut off.

מ ²³The steps of a man are made firm by the LORD,
when He delights in his way.

²⁴Though he stumbles, he does not fall down,
for the LORD gives him support.

נ ²⁵I have been young and am now old,
but I have never seen a righteous man abandoned,
or his children seeking bread.

²⁶He is always generous, and lends,
and his children are held blessed.

ס ²⁷Shun evil and do good,
and you shall abide forever.

²⁸For the LORD loves what is right,
He does not abandon His faithful ones.

They are preserved forever,
while the children of the wicked will be cut off.

²⁹The righteous shall inherit the land,
and abide forever in it.

פ ³⁰The mouth of the righteous utters wisdom,
and his tongue speaks what is right.

ᵇ⁻ᵇ *Lit. "those whose way is upright."*
ᶜ *Lit. "days."*
ᵈ *Meaning of Heb. uncertain.*

³¹The teaching of his God is in his heart;
his feet do not slip.

צ ³²The wicked watches for the righteous,
seeking to put him to death;
³³the LORD will not abandon him to his power;
He will not let him be condemned in judgment.

ק ³⁴Look to the LORD and keep to His way,
and He will raise you high that you may inherit the land;
when the wicked are cut off, you shall see it.

ר ³⁵I saw a wicked man, powerful,
well-rooted like a robust native tree.
³⁶Suddenly he vanished and was gone;
I sought him, but he was not to be found.

ש ³⁷Mark the blameless, note the upright,
for there is a future for the man of integrity.
³⁸But transgressors shall be utterly destroyed,
the future of the wicked shall be cut off.

ת ³⁹The deliverance of the righteous comes from the LORD,
their stronghold in time of trouble.
⁴⁰The LORD helps them and rescues them,
rescues them from the wicked and delivers them,
for they seek refuge in Him.

38 A psalm of David. *Lehazkir.*^a

²O LORD, do not punish me in wrath;
do not chastise me in fury.
³For Your arrows have struck me;
Your blows have fallen upon me.
⁴There is no soundness in my flesh because of Your rage,
no wholeness in my bones because of my sin.
⁵For my iniquities have ^{b-}overwhelmed me;^{-b}
they are like a heavy burden, more than I can bear.
⁶My wounds stink and fester
because of my folly.
⁷I am all bent and bowed;
I walk about in gloom all day long.

---

^a *Meaning of Heb. uncertain.*
^{b-b} *Lit. "passed over my head."*

[8]For my sinews are full of fever;
  there is no soundness in my flesh.
[9]I am all benumbed and crushed;
  I roar because of the turmoil in my mind.

[10]O Lord, You are aware of all my entreaties;
  my groaning is not hidden from You.
[11]My mind reels;
  my strength fails me;
  my eyes too have lost their luster.
[12]My friends and companions stand back from my affliction;
  my kinsmen stand far off.
[13]Those who seek my life lay traps;
  those who wish me harm speak malice;
  they utter deceit all the time.
[14]But I am like a deaf man, unhearing,
  like a dumb man who cannot speak up;
[15]I am like one who does not hear,
  who has no retort on his lips.
[16]But I wait for You, O LORD;
  You will answer, O Lord, my God.
[17]For I fear they will rejoice over me;
  when my foot gives way they will vaunt themselves against
    me.
[18]For I am on the verge of collapse;
  my pain is always with me.
[19]I acknowledge my iniquity;
  I am fearful over my sin;
[20]for my mortal enemies are numerous;
  my treacherous foes are many.
[21]Those who repay evil for good
  harass me for pursuing good.

[22]Do not abandon me, O LORD;
  my God, be not far from me;
  [23]hasten to my aid,
  O Lord, my deliverance.

39 For the leader; for *Jeduthun*. A psalm of David.

²I resolved I would watch my step
    lest I offend by my speech;
    I would keep my mouth muzzled
    while the wicked man was in my presence.
³I was dumb, silent;
    I was very[a] still
    while my pain was intense.
⁴My mind was in a rage,
    my thoughts were all aflame;
    I spoke out:
⁵Tell me, O LORD, what my term is,
    what is the measure of my days;
    I would know how fleeting my life is.
⁶You have made my life just handbreadths long;
    its span is as nothing in Your sight;
    [b-]no man endures any longer than a breath.[-b]   *Selah.*
⁷Man walks about as a mere shadow;
    mere futility is his hustle and bustle,
    amassing and not knowing who will gather in.
⁸What, then, can I count on, O Lord?
In You my hope lies.
⁹Deliver me from all my transgressions;
    make me not the butt of the benighted.
¹⁰I am dumb, I do not speak up,
    for it is Your doing.
¹¹Take away Your plague from me;
    I perish from Your blows.
¹²You chastise a man in punishment for his sin,
    consuming like a moth what he treasures.
No man is more than a breath.   *Selah.*

¹³Hear my prayer, O LORD;
    give ear to my cry;
    do not disregard my tears;

---

[a] *Cf. use of* ṭwb *in Hos. 10.1; Jonah 4.4.*
[b-b] *Meaning of Heb. uncertain.*

for like all my forebears
I am an alien, resident with You.
14Look away from me, b-that I may recover,-b
before I pass away and am gone.

40 For the leader. A psalm of David.

2I put my hope in the LORD;
He inclined toward me,
and heeded my cry.
3He lifted me out of the miry pit,
the slimy clay,
and set my feet on a rock,
steadied my legs.
4He put a new song into my mouth,
a hymn to our God.
May many see it and stand in awe,
and trust in the LORD.
5Happy is the man who makes the LORD his trust,
who turns not to the arrogant or to followers of falsehood.
6 a-You, O LORD my God, have done many things;
the wonders You have devised for us
cannot be set out before You;-a
I would rehearse the tale of them,
but they are more than can be told.
7 b-You gave me to understand that-b
You do not desire sacrifice and meal offering;
You do not ask for burnt offering and sin offering.
8Then I said,
b-"See, I will bring a scroll recounting what befell me."-b
9To do what pleases You, my God, is my desire;
Your teaching is in my inmost parts.
10I proclaimed [Your] righteousness in a great congregation;
see, I did not withhold my words;
O LORD, You must know it.
11I did not keep Your beneficence to myself;

a-a Or "You, O LORD my God, have done many things—/the wonders You have devised for us;/
none can equal You."
b-b Meaning of Heb. uncertain.

I declared Your faithful deliverance;
I did not fail to speak of Your steadfast love in a great
    congregation.
12O LORD, You will not withhold from me Your compassion;
Your steadfast love will protect me always.

13For misfortunes without number envelop me;
my iniquities have caught up with me;
I cannot see;
they are more than the hairs of my head;
c-I am at my wits' end.-c
14 dO favor me, LORD, and save me;
O LORD, hasten to my aid.
15Let those who seek to destroy my life
be frustrated and disgraced;
let those who wish me harm
fall back in shame.
16Let those who say "Aha! Aha!" over me
be desolate because of their frustration.
17But let all who seek You be glad and rejoice in You;
let those who are eager for Your deliverance always say,
"Extolled be the LORD!"
18But I am poor and needy;
may the Lord devise [deliverance] for me.
You are my help and my rescuer;
my God, do not delay.

41 For the leader. A psalm of David.

2Happy is he who is thoughtful of the wretched;
in bad times may the LORD keep him from harm.
3May the LORD guard him and preserve him;
and may he be thought happy in the land.
Do not subject him to the will of his enemies.
4The LORD will sustain him on his sickbed;
a-You shall wholly transform his bed of suffering.-a
5I said, "O LORD, have mercy on me,

c-c Or "my courage fails me."
d With vv. 14–18, cf. Ps. 70.

a-a Meaning of Heb. uncertain.

heal me, for I have sinned against You."
6My enemies speak evilly of me,
  "When will he die and his name perish?"
7If one comes to visit, he speaks falsely;
  his mind stores up evil thoughts;
  once outside, he speaks them.
8All my enemies whisper together against me,
  imagining the worst for me.
9"Something baneful has settled in him;
  he'll not rise from his bed again."
10My ally in whom I trusted,
  even he who shares my bread,
  a-has been utterly false to me.-a
11But You, O LORD, have mercy on me;
  let me rise again and repay them.
12Then shall I know that You are pleased with me:
  when my enemy cannot shout in triumph over me.
13You will support me because of my integrity,
  and let me abide in Your presence forever.

14Blessed is the LORD, God of Israel,
  from eternity to eternity.
  Amen and Amen.

BOOK TWO

42 For the leader. A *maskil* of the Korahites.

2Like a hind crying for water,a
  my soul cries for You, O God;
3my soul thirsts for God, the living God;
  O when will I come to appear before God!
4My tears have been my food day and night;
  I am ever taunted with, "Where is your God?"
5When I think of this, I pour out my soul:

a *Lit. "watercourses."*

how I ^{b-}walked with the crowd, moved with them,^{-b}
   the festive throng, to the House of God
   with joyous shouts of praise.
⁶Why so downcast, my soul,
   why disquieted within me?
Have hope in God;
   I will yet praise Him
   ^{c-}for His saving presence.^{-c}

⁷O my God, my soul is downcast;
   therefore I think of You
in this land of Jordan and Hermon,
   in Mount Mizar,
⁸where deep calls to deep
   in the roar of ^{b-}Your cataracts;^{-b}
all Your breakers and billows have swept over me.
⁹By day may the LORD vouchsafe His faithful care,
   so that at night a song to Him may be with me,
   a prayer to the God of my life.
¹⁰I say to God, my rock,
   "Why have You forgotten me,
   why must I walk in gloom,
   oppressed by my enemy?"
^{11b-}Crushing my bones,^{-b}
   my foes revile me,
   taunting me always with, "Where is your God?"
¹²Why so downcast, my soul,
   why disquieted within me?
Have hope in God;
   I will yet praise Him,
   my ever-present help, my God.

43.

^aVindicate me, O God,
   champion my cause
   against faithless people;
   rescue me from the treacherous, dishonest man.

---

^{b-b} *Meaning of Heb. uncertain.*
^{c-c} *Several ancient versions and Heb. mss. connect the first word in v. 7 with the end of 6, reading*
   yeshu'ot panai we'Elohai, *"my ever-present help, my God," as in vv. 12 and Ps. 43.5.*
^a *A continuation of Ps. 42.*

²For You are my God, my stronghold;
  why have You rejected me?
Why must I walk in gloom,
  oppressed by the enemy?
³Send forth Your light and Your truth;
  they will lead me;
  they will bring me to Your holy mountain,
  to Your dwelling-place,
    ⁴that I may come to the altar of God,
  God, my delight, my joy;
  that I may praise You with the lyre,
  O God, my God.
⁵Why so downcast, my soul,
  why disquieted within me?
Have hope in God;
  I will yet praise Him,
  my ever-present help, my God.

44 For the leader. Of the Korahites. A *maskil*.

²We have heard, O God,
  our fathers have told us
  the deeds You performed in their time,
  in days of old.
³With Your hand You planted them,
  displacing nations;
  You brought misfortune on peoples,
  and drove them out.
⁴It was not by their sword that they took the land,
  their arm did not give them victory,
  but Your right hand, Your arm, and Your goodwill,
  for You favored them.
⁵You are my king, O God;
  decree victories for Jacob!
⁶Through You we gore our foes;
  by Your name we trample our adversaries;

⁷I do not trust in my bow;
  it is not my sword that gives me victory;
⁸You give us victory over our foes;
  You thwart those who hate us.
⁹In God we glory at all times,
  and praise Your name unceasingly.   *Selah.*

¹⁰Yet You have rejected and disgraced us;
  You do not go with our armies.
¹¹You make us retreat before our foe;
  our enemies plunder us at will.
¹²You let them devour us like sheep;
  You disperse us among the nations.
¹³You sell Your people for no fortune,
  You set no high price on them.
¹⁴You make us the butt of our neighbors,
  the scorn and derision of those around us.
¹⁵You make us a byword among the nations,
  a laughingstockᵃ among the peoples.
¹⁶I am always aware of my disgrace;
  I am wholly covered with shame
  ¹⁷at the sound of taunting revilers,
  in the presence of the vengeful foe.

¹⁸All this has come upon us,
  yet we have not forgotten You,
  or been false to Your covenant.
¹⁹Our hearts have not gone astray,
  nor have our feet swerved from Your path,
  ²⁰though You cast us, crushed, to where the ᵇ⁻sea monster⁻ᵇ
    is,
  and covered us over with deepest darkness.
²¹If we forgot the name of our God
  and spread forth our hands to a foreign god,
  ²²God would surely search it out,
  for He knows the secrets of the heart.
²³It is for Your sake that we are slain all day long,
  that we are regarded as sheep to be slaughtered.

ᵃ Lit. *"a wagging of the head."*
ᵇ⁻ᵇ Heb. tannim = tannin, *as in Ezek.* 29.3 *and* 32.2.

²⁴Rouse Yourself; why do You sleep, O Lord?
Awaken, do not reject us forever!
²⁵Why do You hide Your face,
　　ignoring our affliction and distress?
²⁶We lie prostrate in the dust;
　　our body clings to the ground.
²⁷Arise and help us,
　　redeem us, as befits Your faithfulness.

45

For the leader; ᵃ⁻on *shoshannim*.⁻ᵃ Of the Korahites. A *maskil*. A love song.

²My heart is astir with gracious words;
　　I speak my poem to a king;
　　my tongue is the pen of an expert scribe.

³You are fairer than all men;
　　your speech is endowed with grace;
　　rightly has God given you an eternal blessing.
⁴Gird your sword upon your thigh, O hero,
　　in your splendor and glory;
⁵ᵃ⁻in your glory, win success;
　　ride on in the cause of truth and meekness and right;
　　and let your right hand lead you to awesome deeds.⁻ᵃ
⁶Your arrows, sharpened,
　　ᵇ⁻[pierce] the breast of the king's enemies;
　　peoples fall at your feet.⁻ᵇ
⁷Your ᶜ⁻divine throne⁻ᶜ is everlasting;
　　your royal scepter is a scepter of equity.
⁸You love righteousness and hate wickedness;
　　rightly has God, your God, chosen to anoint you
　　with oil of gladness over all your peers.
⁹All your robes [are fragrant] with
　　myrrh and aloes and cassia;
　　from ivoried palaces
　　lutes entertain you.
¹⁰Royal princesses are your favorites;

ᵃ⁻ᵃ *Meaning of Heb. uncertain.*
ᵇ⁻ᵇ *Order of Heb. clauses inverted for clarity.*
ᶜ⁻ᶜ *Cf. 1 Chron. 29.23.*

51

the consort stands at your right hand,
decked in gold of Ophir.

11Take heed, lass, and note,
incline your ear:
forget your people and your father's house,
12and let the king be aroused by your beauty;
since he is your lord, bow to him.
13O Tyrian lass,
the wealthiest people will court your favor with gifts,
14a-goods of all sorts.

The royal princess,
her dress embroidered with golden mountings,
15is led inside to the king;-a
maidens in her train, her companions,
are presented to you.
16They are led in with joy and gladness;
they enter the palace of the king.
17Your sons will succeed your ancestors;
you will appoint them princes throughout the land.

18I commemorate your fame for all generations,
so peoples will praise you forever and ever.

46 For the leader. Of the Korahites; a-on *alamoth.*-a A song.

2God is our refuge and stronghold,
a help in trouble, very near.
3Therefore we are not afraid
though the earth reels,
though mountains topple into the sea—
4its waters rage and foam;
in its swell mountains quake.   *Selah.*

5There is a river whose streams gladden God's city,
the holy dwelling-place of the Most High.

a-a *Meaning of Heb. uncertain.*

52

6God is in its midst, it will not be toppled;
  by daybreak God will come to its aid.
7Nations rage, kingdoms topple;
  at the sound of His thunder the earth dissolves.
8The LORD of hosts is with us;
  the God of Jacob is our haven.   *Selah.*

9Come and see what the LORD has done,
  how He has wrought desolation on the earth.
10He puts a stop to wars throughout the earth,
  breaking the bow, snapping the spear,
  consigning wagons to the flames.
11"Desist! Realize that I am God!
  I dominate the nations;
  I dominate the earth."
12The LORD of hosts is with us;
  the God of Jacob is our haven.   *Selah.*

47 For the leader. Of the Korahites. A psalm.

2All you peoples, clap your hands,
  raise a joyous shout for God.
3For the LORD Most High is awesome,
  great king over all the earth;
    4He subjects peoples to us,
    sets nations at our feet.
5He chose our heritage for us,
  the pride of Jacob whom He loved.   *Selah.*

6God ascends midst acclamation;
  the LORD, to the blasts of the horn.
7Sing, O sing to God;
  sing, O sing to our king;
    8for God is king over all the earth;
    sing a hymn.[a]
9God reigns over the nations;
  God is seated on His holy throne.
10The great of the peoples are gathered together,

---

a *Heb.* maskil, *a musical term of uncertain meaning.*

the retinue of Abraham's God;
for the guardians of the earth belong to God;
He is greatly exalted.

48 A song. A psalm of the Korahites.

²The LORD is great and much acclaimed
in the city of our God,
His holy mountain—
³fair-crested, joy of all the earth,
Mount Zion, summit of Zaphon,ª
city of the great king.
⁴Through its citadels, God has made Himself known as a haven.
⁵See, the kings joined forces;
they advanced together.
⁶At the mere sight of it they were stunned,
they were terrified, they panicked;
⁷they were seized there with a trembling,
like a woman in the throes of labor,
⁸as the Tarshish fleet was wrecked
in an easterly gale.ᵇ
⁹The likes of what we heard we have now witnessed
in the city of the LORD of hosts,
in the city of our God—
may God preserve it forever! *Selah.*

¹⁰In Your temple, God,
we meditate upon Your faithful care.
¹¹The praise of You, God, like Your name,
reaches to the ends of the earth;
Your right hand is filled with beneficence.
¹²Let Mount Zion rejoice!
Let the townsᶜ of Judah exult,
because of Your judgments.

¹³Walk around Zion,
circle it;
count its towers,

ª *A term for the divine abode.*
ᵇ *See 1 Kings 22.49.*
ᶜ *Or "women."*

¹⁴take note of its ramparts;
ᵈ·go through·ᵈ its citadels,
that you may recount it to a future age.
¹⁵For God—He is our God forever;
He will lead us ᵈ·evermore.·ᵈ

49

For the leader. Of the Korahites. A psalm.

²Hear this, all you peoples;
give ear, all inhabitants of the world,
³men of all estates,
rich and poor alike.
⁴My mouth utters wisdom,
my speechᵃ is full of insight.
⁵I will turn my attention to a theme,
set forth my lesson to the music of a lyre.

⁶In time of trouble, why should I fear
the encompassing evil of those who would supplant me—
⁷men who trust in their riches,
who glory in their great wealth?
⁸ᵇ·Ah, it·ᵇ cannot redeem a man,
or pay his ransom to God;
⁹the price of life is too high;
and so one ceases to be, forever.
¹⁰Shall he live eternally,
and never see the grave?
¹¹For one sees that the wise die,
that the foolish and ignorant both perish,
leaving their wealth to others.
¹²Their graveᶜ is their eternal home,
the dwelling-place for all generations
of those once famous on earth.
¹³Man does not abide in honor;
he is like the beasts that perish.

¹⁴Such is the fate of those who are self-confident,
ᵈ·the end of those pleased with their own talk.·ᵈ   *Selah.*

ᵈ⁻ᵈ *Meaning of Heb. uncertain.*
ᵃ *Lit. "utterance of my heart"; on* leb, *cf. Ps. 19.15.*
ᵇ⁻ᵇ *Or "A brother."*
ᶜ *Taken with ancient versions and medieval commentators as the equivalent of* qibram.
ᵈ⁻ᵈ *Meaning of Heb. uncertain.*

¹⁵Sheeplike they head for Sheol,
    with Death as their shepherd.
The upright shall rule over them at daybreak,
    ᵈ⁻and their form shall waste away in Sheol
    till its nobility be gone.⁻ᵈ
¹⁶But God will redeem my life from the clutches of Sheol,
    for He will take me.   *Selah.*

¹⁷Do not be afraid when a man becomes rich,
    when his household goods increase;
    ¹⁸for when he dies he can take none of it along;
    his goods cannot follow him down.
¹⁹Though he congratulates himself in his lifetime
    —ᵈ⁻"They must admit that you did well by yourself"⁻ᵈ—
    ²⁰yet he must join the company of his ancestors,
    who will never see daylight again.
²¹Man does not understand honor;
    he is like the beasts that perish.

50 A psalm of Asaph.

ᵃ⁻God, the LORD God⁻ᵃ spoke
    and summoned the world from east to west.
²From Zion, perfect in beauty,
    God appeared
    ³—let our God come and not fail to act!
Devouring fire preceded Him;
    it stormed around Him fiercely.
⁴He summoned the heavens above,
    and the earth, for the trial of His people.
⁵"Bring in My devotees,
    who made a covenant with Me over sacrifice!"
⁶Then the heavens proclaimed His righteousness,
    for He is a God who judges.   *Selah.*

⁷"Pay heed, My people, and I will speak,
    O Israel, and I will arraign you.

ᵃ⁻ᵃ *Heb.* 'El 'Elohim YHWH.

56

I am God, your God.
⁸I censure you not for your sacrifices,
　　and your burnt offerings, made to Me daily;
　　⁹I claim no bull from your estate,
　　no he-goats from your pens.
¹⁰For Mine is every animal of the forest,
　　the beasts on ᵇ⁻a thousand mountains.⁻ᵇ
¹¹I know every bird of the mountains,
　　the creatures of the field are subject to Me.
¹²Were I hungry, I would not tell you,
　　for Mine is the world and all it holds.
¹³Do I eat the flesh of bulls,
　　or drink the blood of he-goats?
¹⁴Sacrifice a thank offering to God,
　　and pay your vows to the Most High.
¹⁵Call upon Me in time of trouble;
　　I will rescue you, and you shall honor Me."

¹⁶And to the wicked, God said:
　　"Who are you to recite My laws,
　　and mouth the terms of My covenant,
　　¹⁷seeing that you spurn My discipline,
　　and brush My words aside?
¹⁸When you see a thief, you fall in with him,
　　and throw in your lot with adulterers;
　　¹⁹you devote your mouth to evil,
　　and yoke your tongue to deceit;
　　²⁰you are busy maligning your brother,
　　defaming the son of your mother.
²¹If I failed to act when you did these things,
　　you would fancy that I was like you;
　　so I censure you and confront you with charges.
²²Mark this, you who are unmindful of God,
　　lest I tear you apart and no one save you.

²³He who sacrifices a thank offering honors Me,
　　ᵇ⁻and to him who improves his way⁻ᵇ
　　I will show the salvation of God."

ᵇ⁻ᵇ *Meaning of Heb. uncertain.*

51 For the leader. A psalm of David, [2] when Nathan the prophet came to him after he had come to Bathsheba.[a]

[3]Have mercy upon me, O God,
　　as befits Your faithfulness;
　　in keeping with Your abundant compassion,
　　blot out my transgressions.
[4]Wash me thoroughly of my iniquity,
　　and purify me of my sin;
　　[5]for I recognize my transgressions,
　　and am ever conscious of my sin.
[6]Against You alone have I sinned,
　　and done what is evil in Your sight;
　　so You are just in Your sentence,
　　and right in Your judgment.
[7]Indeed I was born with iniquity;
　　with sin my mother conceived me.
[8] [b-]Indeed You desire truth about that which is hidden;
　　teach me wisdom about secret things.[-b]

[9]Purge me with hyssop till I am pure;
　　wash me till I am whiter than snow.
[10]Let me hear tidings of joy and gladness;
　　let the bones You have crushed exult.
[11]Hide Your face from my sins;
　　blot out all my iniquities.
[12]Fashion a pure heart for me, O God;
　　create in me a steadfast spirit.
[13]Do not cast me out of Your presence,
　　or take Your holy spirit away from me.
[14]Let me again rejoice in Your help;
　　let a vigorous spirit sustain me.
[15]I will teach transgressors Your ways,
　　that sinners may return to You.

[16]Save me from bloodguilt,
　　O God, God, my deliverer,

[a] Cf. 2 Sam. 12.
[b-b] Meaning of Heb. uncertain.

that I may sing forth Your beneficence.
17O LORD, open my lips,
  and let my mouth declare Your praise.
18You do not want me to bring sacrifices;
  You do not desire burnt offerings;
19True sacrifice to God is a contrite spirit;
  God, You will not despise
  a contrite and crushed heart.

20May it please You to make Zion prosper;
  rebuild the walls of Jerusalem.
21Then You will want sacrifices offered in righteousness,
  burnt and whole offerings;
  then bulls will be offered on Your altar.

52 For the leader. A *maskil* of David, 2when Doeg the Edomite came and informed Saul, telling him, "David came to Ahimelech's house."[a]

3Why do you boast of your evil, brave fellow?
  God's faithfulness [b-]never ceases.[-b]
4Your tongue devises mischief,
  like a sharpened razor that works treacherously.
5You prefer evil to good,
  the lie, to speaking truthfully.   *Selah.*
6You love all pernicious words,
  treacherous speech.
7So God will tear you down for good,
  will break you and pluck you from your tent,
  and root you out of the land of the living.   *Selah.*
8The righteous, seeing it, will be awestruck;
  they will jibe at him, saying,
9"Here was a fellow who did not make God his refuge,
  but trusted in his great wealth,
  relied upon his mischief."

10But I am like a thriving olive tree in God's house;
  I trust in the faithfulness of God forever and ever.

---

[a] Cf. 1 Sam. 22.9 ff.
[b-b] Lit. "is all the day."

¹¹I praise You forever, for You have acted;
  ^{c-}I declare that Your name is good^{-c}
  in the presence of Your faithful ones.

53

^aFor the leader; on *mahalath.*^b A *maskil* of David.

²The benighted man thinks,
  ^{c-}"God does not care."^{-c}
Man's wrongdoing is corrupt and loathsome;
  no one does good.
³God looks down from heaven on mankind
  to find a man of understanding,
  a man mindful of God.
⁴Everyone is dross,
  altogether foul;
  there is none who does good,
  not even one.
⁵Are they so witless, those evildoers,
  who devour my people as they devour food,
  and do not invoke God?
⁶There they will be seized with fright
  —^{d-}never was there such a fright—
  for God has scattered the bones of your besiegers;
  you have put them to shame,^{-d}
  for God has rejected them.

⁷O that the deliverance of Israel might come from Zion!
When God restores the fortunes of His people,
  Jacob will exult, Israel will rejoice.

54

For the leader; with instrumental music. A *maskil* of David, ²when the Ziphites came and told Saul, "Know, David is in hiding among us."^a

³O God, deliver me by Your name;
  by Your power vindicate me.

---

^{c-c} *Meaning of Heb. uncertain; others "I will wait for Your name for it is good."*

^a *Cf. Ps. 14.*
^b *Meaning of Heb. unknown.*
^{c-c} *Lit. "There is no God"; cf. Ps. 10.4.*
^{d-d} *Meaning of Heb. uncertain.*
^a *Cf. 1 Sam. 23.19.*

⁴O God, hear my prayer;
  give ear to the words of my mouth.
⁵For strangers have risen against me,
  and ruthless men seek my life;
  they are unmindful of God.   *Selah.*

⁶See, God is my helper;
  the LORD is my support.
⁷He will repay the evil of my watchful foes;
  by Your faithfulness, destroy them!
⁸Then I will offer You a freewill sacrifice;
  I will praise Your name, LORD, for it is good,
⁹for it has saved me from my foes,
  and let me gaze triumphant upon my enemies.

55 For the leader; with instrumental music. A *maskil* of David.

²Give ear, O God, to my prayer;
  do not ignore my plea;
  ³pay heed to me and answer me.
I am tossed about, complaining and moaning
  ⁴at the clamor of the enemy,
  because of the oppression of the wicked;
  for they bring evil upon me
  and furiously harass me.
⁵My heart is convulsed within me;
  terrors of death assail me.
⁶Fear and trembling invade me;
  I am clothed with horror.
⁷I said,
  "O that I had the wings of a dove!
  I would fly away and find rest;
  ⁸surely, I would flee far off;
  I would lodge in the wilderness;   *Selah.*
  ⁹I would soon find me a refuge
  from the sweeping wind,
  from the tempest."

¹⁰O LORD, confound their speech, confuse it!
For I see lawlessness and strife in the city;
    ¹¹day and night they make their rounds on its walls;
    evil and mischief are inside it.
¹²Malice is within it;
    fraud and deceit never leave its square.

¹³It is not an enemy who reviles me
    —I could bear that;
    it is not my foe who vaunts himself against me
    —I could hide from him;
    ¹⁴but it is you, my equal,
    my companion, my friend;
    ¹⁵sweet was our fellowship;
    we walked together in God's house.
¹⁶Let Him incite death against them;
    may they go down alive into Sheol!
For where they dwell,
    there evil is.

¹⁷As for me, I call to God;
    the LORD will deliver me.
¹⁸Evening, morning, and noon,
    I complain and moan,
    and He hears my voice.
¹⁹He redeems me unharmed
    from the battle against me;
    ᵃ⁻it is as though many are on my side.⁻ᵃ
²⁰God who has reigned from the first,
    who will have no successor,
    hears and humbles those who have no fear of God.   *Selah.*

²¹Heᵇ harmed his ally,
    he broke his pact;
    ²²his talk was smoother than butter,
    yet his mind was on war;
    his words were more soothing than oil,
    yet they were drawn swords.

ᵃ⁻ᵃ *Meaning of Heb. uncertain.*
ᵇ *I.e., the friend of v. 14.*

62

²³Cast your burden on the LORD and He will sustain you;

He will never let the righteous man collapse.

²⁴For You, O God, will bring them down to the nethermost

Pit—

those murderous, treacherous men;

they shall not live out half their days;

but I trust in You.

56 For the leader; ᵃ⁻on *jonath elem rehokim.*⁻ᵃ Of David. A *michtam*;
when the Philistines seized him in Gath.

²Have mercy on me, O God,

for men persecute me;

all day long my adversary oppresses me.

³My watchful foes persecute me all day long;

many are my adversaries, O Exalted One.

⁴When I am afraid, I trust in You,

⁵in God, whose word I praise,

in God I trust;

I am not afraid;

what can mortalsᵇ do to me?

⁶All day long ᵃ⁻they cause me grief in my affairs,⁻ᵃ

they plan only evil against me.

⁷They plot, they lie in ambush;

they watch my every move, hoping for my death.

⁸Cast them out for their evil;

subdue peoples in Your anger, O God.

⁹ᵃ⁻You keep count of my wanderings;

put my tears into Your flask,

into Your record.⁻ᵃ

¹⁰Then my enemies will retreat when I call on You;

this I know, that God is for me.

¹¹In God, whose word I praise,

in the LORD, whose word I praise,

¹²in God I trust;

I am not afraid;

ᵃ⁻ᵃ *Meaning of Heb. uncertain.*
ᵇ *Lit. "flesh."*

what can man do to me?
13I must pay my vows to You, O God;
I will render thank offerings to You.
14For You have saved me from death,
my foot from stumbling,
that I may walk before God in the light of life.

57

For the leader; a-*al tashheth*.-a Of David. A *michtam*; when he fled from Saul into a cave.

2Have mercy on me, O God, have mercy on me,
for I seek refuge in You,
I seek refuge in the shadow of Your wings,
until danger passes.
3I call to God Most High,
to God who is good to me.
4He will reach down from heaven and deliver me:
God will send down His steadfast love;
my persecutor reviles.   *Selah.*

5As for me, I lie down among man-eating lions
whose teeth are spears and arrows,
whose tongue is a sharp sword.
6Exalt Yourself over the heavens, O God,
let Your glory be over all the earth!
7They prepared a net for my feet b-to ensnare me;-b
they dug a pit for me,
but they fell into it.   *Selah.*

8cMy heart is firm, O God;
my heart is firm;
I will sing, I will chant a hymn.
9Awake, O my soul!
Awake, O harp and lyre!
I will wake the dawn.
10I will praise You among the peoples, O LORD;
I will sing a hymn to You among the nations;

a-a *Meaning of Heb. uncertain.*
b-b *Cf. Mishnaic Heb.* kefifah, *a wicker basket used in fishing.*
c *With vv. 8–12, cf. Ps. 108.2–6.*

64

11for Your faithfulness is as high as heaven;
  Your steadfastness reaches to the sky.
12Exalt Yourself over the heavens, O God,
  let Your glory be over all the earth!

58 For the leader; *al tashheth*. Of David. A *michtam*.

2a-O mighty ones,-a do you really decree what is just?
Do you judge mankind with equity?
3In your minds you devise wrongdoing in the land;
  a-with your hands you deal out lawlessness.-a
4The wicked are defiant from birth;
  the liars go astray from the womb.
5Their venom is like that of a snake,
  a deaf viper that stops its ears
    6so as not to hear the voice of charmers
    or the expert mutterer of spells.

7O God, smash their teeth in their mouth;
  shatter the fangs of lions, O LORD;
    8let them melt, let them vanish like water;
    let Him aim His arrows that they be cut down;
    9a-like a snail that melts away as it moves;-a
    like a woman's stillbirth, may they never see the sun!
10Before a-the thorns grow into a bramble,
  may He whirl them away alive in fury.-a

11The righteous man will rejoice when he sees revenge;
  he will bathe his feet in the blood of the wicked.
12Men will say,
  "There is, then, a reward for the righteous;
  there is, indeed, divine justice on earth."

59 For the leader; *al tashheth*. Of David. A *michtam*; when Saul sent men to watch his house in order to put him to death.a

---

a-a *Meaning of Heb. uncertain.*
a *Cf. 1 Sam. 19.11.*

²Save me from my enemies, O my God;
  secure me against my assailants.
³Save me from evildoers;
  deliver me from murderers.
⁴For see, they lie in wait for me;
  fierce men plot against me
  for no offense of mine,
  for no transgression, O LORD;
⁵for no guilt of mine
  do they rush to array themselves against me.
Look, rouse Yourself on my behalf!
⁶You, O LORD God of hosts,
  God of Israel,
  bestir Yourself to bring all nations to account;
  have no mercy on any treacherous villain.   *Selah.*

⁷They come each evening growling like dogs,
  roaming the city.
⁸They rave with their mouths,
  ᵇ-sharp words-ᵇ are on their lips;
  [they think,] "Who hears?"
⁹But You, O LORD, laugh at them;
  You mock all the nations.

¹⁰O myᶜ strength, I wait for You;
  for God is my haven.
¹¹My faithful God will come to aid me;
  God will let me gloat over my watchful foes.
¹²Do not kill them lest my people be unmindful;
  with Your power make wanderers of them;
  bring them low, O our shield, the Lord,
  ¹³because of their sinful mouths,
  the words on their lips.
Let them be trapped by their pride,
  and by the imprecations and lies they utter.
¹⁴In Your fury put an end to them;
  put an end to them that they be no more;
  that it may be known to the ends of the earth
  that God does rule over Jacob.   *Selah.*

ᵇ⁻ᵇ *Lit. "swords."*
ᶜ *With several mss.; cf. v. 18; lit. "His."*

15They come each evening growling like dogs,
  roaming the city.
16They wander in search of food;
  and whine if they are not satisfied.
17But I will sing of Your strength,
  extol each morning Your faithfulness;
  for You have been my haven,
  a refuge in time of trouble.

18O my strength, to You I sing hymns;
  for God is my haven, my faithful God.

60

For the leader; on a-*shushan eduth*.-a A *michtam* of David (to be taught), 2when he fought with Aram-Naharaim and Aram-Zobah, and Joab returned and defeated Edom—[an army] of twelve thousand men—in the Valley of Salt.b

3O God, You have rejected us,
  You have made a breach in us;
  You have been angry;
  restore us!
4You have made the land quake;
  You have torn it open.
Mend its fissures,
  for it is collapsing.
5You have made Your people suffer hardship;
  c-You have given us wine that makes us reel.-c
6a-Give those who fear You because of Your truth
  a banner for rallying.-a   Selah.
7dThat those whom You love might be rescued,
  deliver with Your right hand and answer me.

8God promised c-in His sanctuary-c
  that I would exultingly divide up Shechem,
  and measure the Valley of Sukkoth;
9Gilead and Manasseh would be mine,
  Ephraim my chief stronghold,
  Judah my scepter;

a-a *Meaning of Heb. uncertain.*
b *Cf. 2 Sam. 8; 1 Chron. 18.*
c-c *Or "You have sated Your people with a bitter draft."*
d *Cf. Ps. 108.7–14.*
e-e *Or "by His holiness."*

¹⁰Moab would be my washbasin;
     on Edom I would cast my shoe;
     acclaim me, O Philistia!

¹¹Would that I were brought to the bastion!
     Would that I were led to Edom!

¹²But You have rejected us, O God;
     God, You do not march with our armies.
¹³Grant us Your aid against the foe,
     for the help of man is worthless.
¹⁴With God we shall triumph;
     He will trample our foes.

61 For the leader; with instrumental music. Of David.

²Hear my cry, O God,
     heed my prayer.
³From the end of the earth I call to You;
     when my heart is faint,
     You lead me to a rock that is high above me.
⁴For You have been my refuge,
     a tower of strength against the enemy.
⁵O that I might dwell in Your tent forever,
     take refuge under Your protecting wings.   *Selah.*

⁶O God, You have heard my vows;
     grant the request[a] of those who fear Your name.
⁷Add days to the days of the king;
     may his years extend through generations;
⁸may he dwell in God's presence forever;
     appoint[b] steadfast love to guard him.
⁹So I will sing hymns to Your name forever,
     as I fulfill my vows day after day.

---

[a] *Taking the noun* yršt *as an alternate form of* 'ršt; *cf. Ps. 21.3.*
[b] *Meaning of Heb. uncertain.*

62 For the leader; on *Jeduthun*. A psalm of David.

²Truly my soul waits quietly for God;
   my deliverance comes from Him.
³Truly He is my rock and deliverance,
   my haven; I shall never be shaken.
⁴How long will all of you attackᵃ a man,
   to crushᵃ him, as though he were
   a leaning wall, a tottering fence?
⁵They lay plans to topple him from his rank;
   they delight in falsehood;
   they bless with their mouths,
   while inwardly they curse.   *Selah*.

⁶Truly, wait quietly for God, O my soul,
   for my hope comes from Him.
⁷He is my rock and deliverance,
   my haven; I shall not be shaken.
⁸I rely on God, my deliverance and glory,
   my rock of strength;
   in God is my refuge.
⁹Trust in Him at all times, O people;
   pour out your hearts before Him;
   God is our refuge.   *Selah*.

¹⁰Men are mere breath;
   mortals, illusion;
   placed on a scale all together,
   they weigh even less than a breath.
¹¹Do not trust in violence,
   or put false hopes in robbery;
   if force bears fruit pay it no mind.
¹²One thing God has spoken;
   two things have I heard:
   that might belongs to God,
   ¹³and faithfulness is Yours, O Lord,
   to reward each man according to his deeds.

ᵃ *Meaning of Heb. uncertain.*

63 A psalm of David, when he was in the Wilderness of Judah.

2God, You are my God;
  I search for You,
  my soul thirsts for You,
  my body yearns for You,
  as a parched and thirsty land that has no water.
3I shall behold You in the sanctuary,
  and see Your might and glory,
4Truly Your faithfulness is better than life;
  my lips declare Your praise.
5I bless You all my life;
  I lift up my hands, invoking Your name.
6I am sated as with a a-rich feast,-a
  I sing praises with joyful lips
7when I call You to mind upon my bed,
  when I think of You in the watches of the night;
8for You are my help,
  and in the shadow of Your wings
  I shout for joy.
9My soul is attached to You;
  Your right hand supports me.

10May those who seek to destroy my life
  enter the depths of the earth.
11May they be gutted by the sword;
  may they be prey to jackals.
12But the king shall rejoice in God;
  all who swear by Him shall exult,
  when the mouth of liars is stopped.

64 For the leader. A psalm of David.

2Hear my voice, O God, when I plead;
  guard my life from the enemy's terror.
3Hide me from a band of evil men,

a-a Lit. "suet and fat."

from a crowd of evildoers,
⁴who whet their tongues like swords;
they aim their arrows—cruel words—
⁵to shoot from hiding at the blameless man;
they shoot him suddenly and without fear.
⁶ᵃ·They arm themselves with an evil word;
when they speak, it is to conceal traps;⁻ᵃ
they think, "Who will see them?"
⁷ᵇLet the wrongdoings they have concealed,ᶜ
each one inside him, his secret thoughts,
be wholly exposed.
⁸God shall shoot them with arrows;
they shall be struck down suddenly.
⁹Their tongue shall be their downfall;
all who see them shall recoil in horror;
¹⁰all men shall stand in awe;
they shall proclaim the work of God
and His deed which they perceived.
¹¹The righteous shall rejoice in the LORD,
and take refuge in Him;
all the upright shall exult.

65

For the leader. A psalm of David. A song.

²Praise befits You in Zion, O God;
vows are paid to You;
³all mankindᵃ comes to You,
You who hear prayer.
⁴When all manner of sins overwhelm me,
it is You who forgive our iniquities.
⁵Happy is the man You choose and bring near
to dwell in Your courts;
may we be sated with the blessings of Your house,
Your holy temple.

⁶Answer us with victory through awesome deeds,
O God, our deliverer,

ᵃ⁻ᵃ *Meaning of Heb. uncertain.*
ᵇ *Meaning of verse uncertain.*
ᶜ *Reading* ṭamnu *with some mss. (cf. Minḥat Shai) and Rashi; most printed editions,* támnu *traditionally rendered "they have accomplished."*

ᵃ *Lit. "flesh."*

in whom all the ends of the earth
and the distant seas
put their trust;
7who by His power fixed the mountains firmly,
who is girded with might,
8who stills the raging seas,
the raging waves,
and tumultuous peoples.
9Those who live at the ends of the earth are awed by Your signs;
You make the lands of sunrise and sunset shout for joy.
10You take care of the earth and irrigate it;
You enrich it greatly,
with the channel of God full of water;
You provide grain for men;
for so do You prepare it.
11Saturating its furrows,
leveling its ridges,
You soften it with showers,
You bless its growth.
12You crown the year with Your bounty;
fatness is distilled in Your paths;
13the pasturelands distill it;
the hills are girded with joy.
14The meadows are clothed with flocks,
the valleys mantled with grain;
they raise a shout, they break into song.

66 For the leader. A song. A psalm.

2Raise a shout for God, all the earth;
sing the glory of His name,
make glorious His praise.
3Say to God,
"How awesome are Your deeds,
Your enemies cower before Your great strength;
4all the earth bows to You,

and sings hymns to You;
all sing hymns to Your name."   *Selah.*

5Come and see the works of God,
    who is held in awe by men for His acts.
6He turned the sea into dry land;
    they crossed the river on foot;
    we therefore rejoice in Him.
7He rules forever in His might;
    His eyes scan the nations;
    let the rebellious not assert themselves.   *Selah.*

8O peoples, bless our God,
    celebrate His praises;
    9who has granted us life,
    and has not let our feet slip.

10You have tried us, O God,
    refining us, as one refines silver.
11You have caught us in a net,
    a-caught us in trammels.-a
12You have let men ride over us;
    we have endured fire and water,
    and You have brought us through to prosperity.

13I enter Your house with burnt offerings,
    I pay my vows to You,
    14[vows] that my lips pronounced,
    that my mouth uttered in my distress.
15I offer up fatlings to You,
    with the odor of burning rams;
    I sacrifice bulls and he-goats.   *Selah.*

·16Come and hear, all God-fearing men,
    as I tell what He did for me.
17I called aloud to Him,
    glorification on my tongue.

a-a Lit. *"put a trammel on our loins."*

¹⁸Had I an evil thought in my mind,
    the LORD would not have listened.
¹⁹But God did listen;
    He paid heed to my prayer.
²⁰Blessed is God who has not turned away my prayer,
    or His faithful care from me.

67 For the leader; with instrumental music. A psalm. A song.

²May God be gracious to us and bless us;
    may He show us favor,   *Selah.*
³that Your way be known on earth,
    Your deliverance among all nations.

⁴Peoples will praise You, O God;
    all peoples will praise You.
⁵Nations will exult and shout for joy,
    for You rule the peoples with equity,
    You guide the nations of the earth.   *Selah.*
⁶The peoples will praise You, O God;
    all peoples will praise You.

⁷May the earth yield its produce;
    may God, our God, bless us.
⁸May God bless us,
    and be revered to the ends of the earth.

68 ᵃFor the leader. Of David. A psalm. A song.

²God will arise,
    His enemies shall be scattered,
    His foes shall flee before Him.
³Disperse them as smoke is dispersed;
    as wax melts at fire,
    so the wicked shall perish before God.
⁴But the righteous shall rejoice;

ᵃ *The coherence of this psalm and the meaning of many of its passages are uncertain.*

they shall exult in the presence of God;
they shall be exceedingly joyful.

5Sing to God, chant hymns to His name;
extol Him who rides the clouds;
the LORD is His name.
Exult in His presence—
6the father of orphans, the champion of widows,
God, in His holy habitation.
7God restores the lonely to their homes,
sets free the imprisoned, safe and sound,
while the rebellious must live in a parched land.

8O God, when You went at the head of Your army,
when You marched through the desert,   *Selah.*
9the earth trembled, the sky rained because of God,
yon Sinai, because of God, the God of Israel.
10You released a bountiful rain, O God;
when Your own land languished, You sustained it.
11Your tribe dwells there;
O God, in Your goodness You provide for the needy.

12The LORD gives a command;
the women who bring the news are a great host:
13"The kings and their armies are in headlong flight;
housewives are sharing in the spoils;
14even for those of you who lie among the sheepfolds
there are wings of a dove sheathed in silver,
its pinions in fine gold."
15When Shaddai scattered the kings,
it seemed like a snowstorm in Zalmon.

16O majestic mountain, Mount Bashan;
O jagged mountain, Mount Bashan;
17why so hostile, O jagged mountains,
toward the mountain God desired as His dwelling?
The LORD shall abide there forever.

¹⁸God's chariots are myriads upon myriads,
thousands upon thousands;
the Lord is among them as in Sinai in holiness.

¹⁹You went up to the heights, having taken captives,
having received tribute of men,
even of those who rebel
against the LORD God's abiding there.

²⁰Blessed is the LORD.
Day by day He supports us,
God, our deliverance.   *Selah*.
²¹God is for us a God of deliverance;
GOD the Lord provides an escape from death.
²²God will smash the heads of His enemies,
the hairy crown of him who walks about in his guilt.
²³The LORD said, "I will retrieve from Bashan,
I will retrieve from the depths of the sea;
²⁴that your feet may wade through blood;
that the tongue of your dogs may have its portion of your
enemies."

²⁵Men see Your processions, O God,
the processions of my God, my king,
into the sanctuary.
²⁶First come singers, then musicians,
amidst maidens playing timbrels.
²⁷In assemblies bless God,
the LORD, O you who are from the fountain of Israel.
²⁸There is little Benjamin who rules them,
the princes of Judah who command them,
the princes of Zebulun and Naphtali.

²⁹Your God has ordained strength for you,
the strength, O God,
which You displayed for us
³⁰from Your temple above Jerusalem.
The kings bring You tribute.

³¹Blast the beast of the marsh,
　　the herd of bulls among the peoples, the calves,
　　till they come cringing with pieces of silver.
Scatter the peoples who delight in wars!
³²Tribute-bearers shall come from Egypt;
　　Cush shall hasten its gifts to God.

³³O kingdoms of the earth,
　　sing to God;
　　chant hymns to the Lord,　　　　　　　　　　　*Selah.*
　　³⁴to Him who rides the ancient highest heavens,
　　who thunders forth with His mighty voice.
³⁵Ascribe might to God,
　　whose majesty is over Israel,
　　whose might is in the skies.
³⁶You are awesome, O God, in Your holy places;
　　it is the God of Israel who gives might and power to the
　　　　people.
Blessed is God.

69 For the leader. On *shoshannim.*ᵃ Of David.

²Deliver me, O God,
　　for the waters have reached my neck;
　　³I am sinking into the slimy deep
　　and find no foothold;
　　I have come into the watery depths;
　　the flood sweeps me away.
⁴I am weary with calling;
　　my throat is dry;
　　my eyes fail
　　while I wait for God.
⁵More numerous than the hairs of my head
　　are those who hate me without reason;
　　many are those who would destroy me,
　　my treacherous enemies.
Must I restore what I have not stolen?

ᵃ *Meaning of Heb. uncertain.*

⁶God, You know my folly;
    my guilty deeds are not hidden from You.
⁷Let those who look to You,
    O LORD, God of hosts,
    not be disappointed on my account;
    let those who seek You,
    O God of Israel,
    not be shamed because of me.
⁸It is for Your sake that I have been reviled,
    that shame covers my face;
    ⁹I am a stranger to my brothers,
    an alien to my kin.
¹⁰My zeal for Your house has been my undoing;
    the reproaches of those who revile You have fallen upon me.
¹¹When I wept and fasted,
    I was reviled for it.
¹²I made sackcloth my garment;
    I became a byword among them.
¹³Those who sit in the gate talk about me;
    I am the taunt of drunkards.

¹⁴As for me, may my prayer come to You, O LORD,
    at a favorable moment;
    O God, in Your abundant faithfulness,
    answer me with Your sure deliverance.
¹⁵Rescue me from the mire;
    let me not sink;
    let me be rescued from my enemies,
    and from the watery depths.
¹⁶Let the floodwaters not sweep me away;
    let the deep not swallow me;
    let the mouth of the Pit not close over me.
¹⁷Answer me, O LORD,
    according to Your great steadfastness;
    in accordance with Your abundant mercy
    turn to me;
    ¹⁸do not hide Your face from Your servant,
    for I am in distress;

answer me quickly.
19Come near to me and redeem me;
 free me from my enemies.

20You know my reproach,
 my shame, my disgrace;
 You are aware of all my foes.
21Reproach breaks my heart,
 I am in despair;ᵃ
 I hope for consolation, but there is none,
 for comforters, but find none.
22They give me gall for food,
 vinegar to quench my thirst.
23May their table be a trap for them,
 a snare for their allies.
24May their eyes grow dim so that they cannot see;
 may their loins collapse continually.
25Pour out Your wrath on them;
 may Your blazing anger overtake them;
 26may their encampments be desolate;
 may their tents stand empty.
27For they persecute those You have struck;
 they talk about the pain of those You have felled.
28Add that to their guilt;
 let them have no share of Your beneficence;
 29may they be erased from the book of life,
 and not be inscribed with the righteous.

30But I am lowly and in pain;
 Your help, O God, keeps me safe.
31I will extol God's name with song,
 and exalt Him with praise.
32That will please the LORD more than oxen,
 than bulls with horns and hooves.
33The lowly will see and rejoice;
 you who are mindful of God, take heart!
34For the LORD listens to the needy,
 and does not spurn His captives.

³⁵Heaven and earth shall extol Him,
the seas, and all that moves in them.
³⁶For God will deliver Zion
and rebuild the cities of Judah;
they shall live there and inherit it;
³⁷the offspring of His servants shall possess it;
those who cherish His name shall dwell there.

70

For the leader. Of David. *Lehazkir*.^a

^{2b}Hasten, O God, to save me;
O LORD, to aid me!
³Let those who seek my life
be frustrated and disgraced;
let those who wish me harm,
fall back in shame.
⁴Let those who say, "Aha! Aha!"
turn back because of their frustration.

⁵But let all who seek You be glad and rejoice in You;
let those who are eager for Your deliverance always say,
"Extolled be God!"
⁶But I am poor and needy;
O God, hasten to me!
You are my help and my rescuer;
O LORD, do not delay.

71

I seek refuge in You, O LORD;
may I never be disappointed.
²As You are beneficent, save me and rescue me;
incline Your ear to me and deliver me.
³Be a sheltering rock for me to which I may always repair;
decree my deliverance,
for You are my rock and my fortress.
⁴My God, rescue me from the hand of the wicked,
from the grasp of the unjust and the lawless.

---

^a *Meaning of Heb. uncertain.*
^b *Cf. Ps. 40.14–18.*

⁵For You are my hope,
  O Lord GOD,
  my trust from my youth.
⁶While yet unborn, I depended on You;
  in the womb of my mother, You were my support;ᵃ
  I sing Your praises always.
⁷I have become an example for many,
  since You are my mighty refuge.
⁸My mouth is full of praise to You,
  glorifying You all day long.
⁹Do not cast me off in old age;
  when my strength fails, do not forsake me!

¹⁰For my enemies talk against me;
  those who wait for me are of one mind,
  ¹¹saying, "God has forsaken him;
  chase him and catch him,
  for no one will save him!"
¹²O God, be not far from me;
  my God, hasten to my aid!
¹³Let my accusers perish in frustration;
  let those who seek my ruin be clothed in reproach and
    disgrace!

¹⁴As for me, I will hope always,
  and add to the many praises of You.
¹⁵My mouth tells of Your beneficence,
  of Your deliverance all day long,
  though I know not how to tell it.
¹⁶I come with praise of Your mighty acts, O Lord GOD;
  I celebrate Your beneficence, Yours alone.
¹⁷You have let me experience it, God, from my youth;
  until now I have proclaimed Your wondrous deeds,
  ¹⁸and even in hoary old age do not forsake me, God,
  until I proclaim Your strength to the next generation,
  ¹⁹Your mighty acts, to all who are to come,
  Your beneficence, high as the heavens, O God,
  You who have done great things;

ᵃ *Meaning of Heb. uncertain.*

O God, who is Your peer!
²⁰You who have made me undergo many troubles and
   misfortunes
   will revive me again,
   and raise me up from the depths of the earth.
²¹You will grant me much greatness,
   You will turn and comfort me.
²²Then I will acclaim You to the music of the lyre
   for Your faithfulness, O my God;
   I will sing a hymn to You with a harp,
   O Holy One of Israel.
²³My lips shall be jubilant, as I sing a hymn to You,
   my whole being, which You have redeemed.
²⁴All day long my tongue shall recite Your beneficent acts,
   how those who sought my ruin were frustrated and
   disgraced.

72 Of Solomon.

O God, endow the king with Your judgments,
   the king's son with Your righteousness;
²that he may judge Your people rightly,
   Your lowly ones, justly.
³Let the mountains produce well-being for the people,
   the hills, the reward of justice.
⁴Let him champion the lowly among the people,
   deliver the needy folk,
   and crush those who wrong them.
⁵Let them fear You as long as the sun shines,
   while the moon lasts, generations on end.
⁶Let him be like rain that falls on a mown field,
   like a downpour of rain on the ground,
⁷that the righteous may flourish in his time,
   and well-being abound, till the moon is no more.
⁸Let him rule from sea to sea,
   from the river to the ends of the earth.

⁹Let desert-dwellers kneel before him,
   and his enemies lick the dust.
¹⁰Let kings of Tarshish and the islands pay tribute,
   kings of Sheba and Seba offer gifts.
¹¹Let all kings bow to him,
   and all nations serve him.

¹²For he saves the needy who cry out,
   the lowly who have no helper.
¹³He cares about the poor and the needy;
   He brings the needy deliverance.
¹⁴He redeems them from fraud and lawlessness;
   ᵃ⁻the shedding of their blood weighs heavily upon him.⁻ᵃ

¹⁵So let him live, and receive gold of Sheba;
   let prayers for him be said always,
   blessings on him invoked at all times.
¹⁶ᵇ⁻Let abundant grain be in the land, to the tops of the
         mountains;
   let his crops thrive like the forest of Lebanon;
   and let men sprout up in towns like country grass.
¹⁷May his name be eternal;
   while the sun lasts, may his name endure;⁻ᵇ
   let men invoke his blessedness upon themselves;
   let all nations count him happy.

¹⁸Blessed is the LORD God, God of Israel,
   who alone does wondrous things;
¹⁹Blessed is His glorious name forever;
   His glory fills the whole world.
   Amen and Amen.

²⁰End of the prayers of David son of Jesse.

ᵃ⁻ᵃ *Or "their life is precious in his sight."*
ᵇ⁻ᵇ *Meaning of some Heb. phrases in these verses uncertain.*

BOOK THREE

73 A psalm of Asaph.

God is truly good to Israel,
to those whose heart is pure.
²As for me, my feet had almost strayed,
my steps were nearly led off course,
³for I envied the wanton;
I saw the wicked at ease.
⁴Death has no pangs for them;
their body is healthy.
⁵They have no part in the travail of men;
they are not afflicted like the rest of mankind.
⁶So pride adorns their necks,
lawlessness enwraps them as a mantle.
⁷ᵃ·Fat shuts out their eyes;
their fancies are extravagant.·ᵃ
⁸They scoff and plan evil;
from their eminence they plan wrongdoing.
⁹They set their mouths against heaven,
and their tongues range over the earth.
¹⁰ᵃ·So they pound His people again and again,
until they are drained of their very last tear.·ᵃ
¹¹Then they say, "How could God know?
Is there knowledge with the Most High?"
¹²Such are the wicked;
ever tranquil, they amass wealth.

¹³It was for nothing that I kept my heart pure
and washed my hands in innocence,
¹⁴seeing that I have been constantly afflicted,
that each morning brings new punishments.
¹⁵Had I decided to say these things,
I should have been false to the circle of Your disciples.
¹⁶So I applied myself to understand this,
but it seemed a hopeless task

ᵃ·ᵃ *Meaning of Heb. uncertain.*

17till I entered God's sanctuary
and reflected on their fate.

18You surround them with flattery;
You make them fall through blandishments.
19How suddenly are they ruined,
wholly swept away by terrors.
20a·When You are aroused You despise their image,
as one does a dream after waking, O LORD.·a

21My mind was stripped of its reason,
b·my feelings were numbed.·b
22I was a dolt, without knowledge;
I was brutish toward You.

23Yet I was always with You,
You held my right hand;
24You guided me by Your counsel
c·and led me toward honor.·c
25Whom else have I in heaven?
And having You, I want no one on earth.
26My body and mind fail;
but God is the stayd of my mind, my portion forever.
27Those who keep far from You perish;
You annihilate all who are untrue to You.
28As for me, nearness to God is good;
I have made the Lord GOD my refuge,
that I may recount all Your works.

74 A *maskil* of Asaph.

Why, O God, do You forever reject us,
do You fume in anger at the flock that You tend?
2Remember the community You made Yours long ago,
Your very own tribe that You redeemed,
Mount Zion, where You dwell.
3a·Bestir Yourself·a because of the b·perpetual tumult,·b

b-b Lit. "I was pierced through in my kidneys."
c-c Meaning of Heb. uncertain; others "And afterward receive me with glory."
d Lit. "rock."

a-a Lit. "Lift up Your feet."
b-b Meaning of Heb. uncertain.

all the outrages of the enemy in the sanctuary.
4Your foes roar inside Your meeting-place;
 they take their signs for true signs.
5b-It is like men wielding axes
 against a gnarled tree;
 6with hatchet and pike
 they hacked away at its carved work.-b.
7They made Your sanctuary go up in flames;
 they brought low in dishonor the dwelling-place of Your
 presence.
8They resolved, "Let us destroy them altogether!"
 They burned all God's tabernacles in the land.
9No signs appear for us;
 there is no longer any prophet;
 no one among us knows for how long.

10Till when, O God, will the foe blaspheme,
 will the enemy forever revile Your name?
11Why do You hold back Your hand, Your right hand?
b-Draw it out of Your bosom!-b

12O God, my king from of old,
 who brings deliverance throughout the land;
 13it was You who drove back the sea with Your might,
 who smashed the heads of the monsters in the waters;
 14it was You who crushed the heads of Leviathan,
 who left him as food for c-the denizens of the desert;-c
 15it was You who released springs and torrents,
 who made mighty rivers run dry;
 16the day is Yours, the night also;
 it was You who set in place the orb of the sun;
 17You fixed all the boundaries of the earth;
 summer and winter—You made them.

18Be mindful of how the enemy blasphemes the LORD,
 how base people revile Your name.
19Do not deliver Your dove to the wild beast;

c-c Or "seafaring men"; meaning of Heb. uncertain.

do not ignore forever the band of Your lowly ones.
20Look to the covenant!
For the dark places of the land are full of the haunts of
lawlessness.
21Let not the downtrodden turn away disappointed;
let the poor and needy praise Your name.
22Rise, O God, champion Your cause;
be mindful that You are blasphemed by base men all day
long.
23Do not ignore the shouts of Your foes,
the din of Your adversaries that ascends all the time.

75 For the leader; *al tashheth*.
A psalm of Asaph, a song.

2We praise You, O God;
we praise You;
Your presence is near;
men tell of Your wondrous deeds.

3"At the time I choose,
I will give judgment equitably.
4Earth and all its inhabitants dissolve;
it is I who keep its pillars firm.   *Selah.*
5To wanton men I say, 'Do not be wanton!'
to the wicked, 'Do not lift up your horns!' "

6Do not lift your horns up high
a-in vainglorious bluster.-a
7For what lifts a man comes not from the east
or the west or the wilderness;b
8for God it is who gives judgment;
He brings down one man, He lifts up another.
9There is a cup in the LORD's hand
with foaming wine fully mixed;
from this He pours;

---

a-a *Lit.* "with arrogant neck you speak."
b *Reading* midbār *with many mss.*

all the wicked of the earth drink,
    draining it to the very dregs.
¹⁰As for me, I will declare forever,
    I will sing a hymn to the God of Jacob.

¹¹"All the horns of the wicked I will cut;
    but the horns of the righteous shall be lifted up."

76 For the leader; with instrumental music.
A psalm of Asaph, a song.

²God has made Himself known in Judah,
    His name is great in Israel;
    ³Salem became His abode;
    Zion, His den.
⁴There He broke the fiery arrows of the bow,
    the shield and the sword of war.   *Selah.*

⁵You were resplendent,
    glorious, on the mountains of prey.
⁶The stout-hearted were despoiled;
    they were in a stupor;
    the bravest of men could not lift a hand.
⁷At Your blast, O God of Jacob,
    horse and chariot lay stunned.
⁸O You! You are awesome!
Who can withstand You
    when You are enraged?
⁹In heaven You pronounced sentence;
    the earth was numbed with fright
    ¹⁰as God rose to execute judgment,
    to deliver all the lowly of the earth.   *Selah.*

¹¹ᵃ⁻The fiercest of men shall acknowledge You,
    when You gird on the last bit of fury.⁻ᵃ
¹²Make vows and pay them to the LORD your God;

ᵃ⁻ᵃ *Meaning of Heb. uncertain.*

ᵃ⁻all who are around Him shall bring tribute to
    the Awesome One.⁻ᵃ
¹³He curbs the spirit of princes,
    inspires awe in the kings of the earth.

77 For the leader; on *Jeduthun*. Of Asaph. A psalm.

²I cry aloud to God;
    I cry to God that He may give ear to me.
³In my time of distress I turn to the Lord,
    ᵃ⁻with my hand [uplifted];
    [my eyes] flow all night without respite;⁻ᵃ
    I will not be comforted.
⁴I call God to mind, I moan,
    I complain, my spirit fails.   *Selah.*

⁵You have held my eyelids open;
    I am overwrought, I cannot speak.
⁶My thoughts turn to days of old,
    to years long past.
⁷I recall at night their jibes at me;
    I commune with myself;
    my spirit inquires,
⁸"Will the Lord reject forever
    and never again show favor?
⁹Has His faithfulness disappeared forever?
Will His promise be unfulfilled for all time?
¹⁰Has God forgotten how to pity?
Has He in anger stifled His compassion?"   *Selah.*
¹¹And I said, ᵃ⁻"It is my fault
    that the right hand of the Most High has changed."⁻ᵃ

¹²I recall the deeds of the LORD;
    yes, I recall Your wonders of old;
    ¹³I recount all Your works;

ᵃ⁻ᵃ *Meaning of Heb. uncertain.*

I speak of Your acts.
14O God, Your ways are holiness;
    what god is as great as God?
15You are the God who works wonders;
    You have manifested Your strength among the peoples.
16By Your arm You redeemed Your people,
    the children of Jacob and Joseph.   *Selah.*
17The waters saw You, O God,
    the waters saw You and were convulsed;
    the very deep quaked as well.
18Clouds streamed water;
    the heavens rumbled;
    Your arrows flew about;
19Your thunder rumbled like wheels;
    lightning lit up the world;
    the earth quaked and trembled.
20Your way was through the sea,
    Your path, through the mighty waters;
    Your tracks could not be seen.
21You led Your people like a flock
    in the care of Moses and Aaron.

78 A *maskil* of Asaph.

Give ear, my people, to my teaching,
    turn your ear to what I say.
2I will expound a theme,
    hold forth on the lessons of the past,
3things we have heard and known,
    that our fathers have told us.
4We will not withhold them from their children,
    telling the coming generation
    the praises of the LORD and His might,
    and the wonders He performed.
5He established a decree in Jacob,
    ordained a teaching in Israel,
    charging our fathers

to make them known to their children,
⁶that a future generation might know
—children yet to be born—
and in turn tell their children
⁷that they might put their confidence in God,
and not forget God's great deeds,
but observe His commandments,
⁸and not be like their fathers,
a wayward and defiant generation,
a generation whose heart was inconstant,
whose spirit was not true to God.

⁹Like the Ephraimite bowmen
who played false in the day of battle,
¹⁰they did not keep God's covenant,
they refused to follow His instruction;
¹¹they forgot His deeds
and the wonders that He showed them.
¹²He performed marvels in the sight of their fathers,
in the land of Egypt, the plain of Zoan.
¹³He split the sea and took them through it;
He made the waters stand like a wall.
¹⁴He led them with a cloud by day,
and throughout the night by the light of fire.
¹⁵He split rocks in the wilderness
and gave them drink as if from the great deep.
¹⁶He brought forth streams from a rock
and made them flow down like a river.

¹⁷But they went on sinning against Him,
defying the Most High in the parched land.
¹⁸To test God was in their mind
when they demanded food for themselves.
¹⁹They spoke against God, saying,
"Can God spread a feast in the wilderness?
²⁰True, He struck the rock and waters flowed,
streams gushed forth;

but can He provide bread?
Can He supply His people with meat?"
²¹The LORD heard and He raged;
 fire broke out against Jacob,
 anger flared up at Israel,
  ²²because they did not put their trust in God,
  did not rely on His deliverance.
²³So He commanded the skies above,
 He opened the doors of heaven
  ²⁴and rained manna upon them for food,
  giving them heavenly grain.
²⁵Each man ate a hero's meal;
 He sent them provision in plenty.
²⁶He set the east wind moving in heaven,
 and drove the south wind by His might.
²⁷He rained meat on them like dust,
 winged birds like the sands of the sea,
  ²⁸making them come down inside His camp,
  around His dwelling-place.
²⁹They ate till they were sated;
 He gave them what they craved.
³⁰They had not yet wearied of what they craved,
 the food was still in their mouths
  ³¹when God's anger flared up at them.
He slew their sturdiest,
 struck down the youth of Israel.
³²Nonetheless, they went on sinning
 and had no faith in His wonders.
³³He made their days end in futility,
 their years in sudden death.
³⁴When He struckᵃ them, they turned to Him
 and sought God once again.
³⁵They remembered that God was their rock,
 God Most High, their Redeemer.
³⁶Yet they deceived Him with their speech,
 lied to Him with their words;
  ³⁷their hearts were inconstant toward Him;

 ᵃ *Lit. "killed."*

they were untrue to His covenant.
38But He, being merciful, forgave iniquity
and would not destroy;
He restrained His wrath time and again
and did not give full vent to His fury;
39for He remembered that they were but flesh,
a passing breath that does not return.

40How often did they defy Him in the wilderness,
did they grieve Him in the wasteland!
41Again and again they tested God,
vexedb the Holy One of Israel.
42They did not remember His strength,
or the day He redeemed them from the foe;
43how He displayed His signs in Egypt,
His wonders in the plain of Zoan.
44He turned their rivers into blood;
He made their waters undrinkable.
45He inflicted upon them swarms of insects to devour them,
frogs to destroy them.
46He gave their crops over to grubs,
their produce to locusts.
47He killed their vines with hail,
their sycamores c-with frost.-c
48He gave their beasts over to hail,
their cattle to lightning bolts.
49He inflicted His burning anger upon them,
wrath, indignation, trouble,
a band of deadly messengers.
50He cleared a path for His anger;
He did not stop short of slaying them,
but gave them over to pestilence.
51He struck every first-born in Egypt,
the first fruits of their vigor in the tents of Ham.
52He set His people moving like sheep,
drove them like a flock in the wilderness.
53He led them in safety; they were unafraid;

b Or "set a limit to."
c-c Meaning of Heb. uncertain.

as for their enemies, the sea covered them.

⁵⁴He brought them to His holy realm,ᵈ
　　the mountain His right hand had acquired.

⁵⁵He expelled nations before them,
　　ᶜ⁻settled the tribes of Israel in their tents,
　　allotting them their portion by the line.⁻ᶜ

⁵⁶Yet they defiantly tested God Most High,
　　and did not observe His decrees.

⁵⁷They fell away, disloyal like their fathers;
　　they played false like a treacherous bow.

⁵⁸They vexed Him with their high places;
　　they incensed Him with their idols.

⁵⁹God heard it and was enraged;
　　He utterly rejected Israel.

⁶⁰He forsook the tabernacle of Shiloh,
　　the tent He had set among men.

⁶¹He let His mightᶠ go into captivity,
　　His glory into the hands of the foe.

⁶²He gave His people over to the sword;
　　He was enraged at His very own.

⁶³Fire consumed their young men,
　　and their maidens ᵍ⁻remained unwed.⁻ᵍ

⁶⁴Their priests fell by the sword,
　　and their widows could not weep.

⁶⁵The Lord awoke as from sleep,
　　like a warrior ᶜ⁻shaking off⁻ᶜ wine.

⁶⁶He beat back His foes,
　　dealing them lasting disgrace.

⁶⁷He rejected the clan of Joseph;
　　He did not choose the tribe of Ephraim.

⁶⁸He did choose the tribe of Judah,
　　Mount Zion, which He loved.

⁶⁹He built His Sanctuary like the heavens,
　　like the earth that He established forever.

⁷⁰He chose David, His servant,
　　and took him from the sheepfolds.

ᵈ Or "hill" with Septuagint and Saadia.
ᶜ⁻ᶜ Inverted for clarity.
ᶠ I.e., the Ark; cf. Ps. 132.8.
ᵍ⁻ᵍ Lit. "had no nuptial song."

71He brought him from minding the nursing ewes
  to tend His people Jacob, Israel, His very own.
72He tended them with blameless heart;
  with skillful hands he led them.

79 A psalm of Asaph.

O God, heathens have entered Your domain,
  defiled Your holy temple,
  and turned Jerusalem into ruins.
2They have left Your servants' corpses
  as food for the fowl of heaven,
  and the flesh of Your faithful for the wild beasts.
3Their blood was shed like water around Jerusalem,
  with none to bury them.
4We have become the butt of our neighbors,
  the scorn and derision of those around us.

5How long, O LORD, will You be angry forever,
  will Your indignation blaze like fire?
6Pour out Your fury on the nations that do not know You,
  upon the kingdoms that do not invoke Your name,
7for they have devoured Jacob
  and desolated his home.
8Do not hold our former iniquities against us;
  let Your compassion come swiftly toward us,
  for we have sunk very low.
9Help us, O God, our deliverer,
  for the sake of the glory of Your name.
Save us and forgive our sin,
  for the sake of Your name.
10Let the nations not say, "Where is their God?"
Before our eyes let it be known among the nations
  that You avenge the spilled blood of Your servants.
11Let the groans of the prisoners reach You;
  reprieve those condemned to death,
  as befits Your great strength.

12Pay back our neighbors sevenfold
  for the abuse they have flung at You, O LORD.
13Then we, Your people,
  the flock You shepherd,
  shall glorify You forever;
  for all time we shall tell Your praises.

80 For the leader; on *shoshannim, eduth*. Of Asaph. A psalm.

2Give ear, O shepherd of Israel
  who leads Joseph like a flock!
Appear, You who are enthroned on the cherubim,
  3at the head of Ephraim, Benjamin, and Manasseh!
Rouse Your might and come to our help!
4Restore us, O God;
  show Your favor that we may be delivered.

5O LORD, God of hosts,
  how long will You be wrathful
  toward the prayers of Your people?
6You have fed them tears as their daily bread,
  made them drink great measures of tears.
7You set us at strife with our neighbors;
  our enemies mock us at will.
8O God of hosts, restore us;
  show Your favor that we may be delivered.

9You plucked up a vine from Egypt;
  You expelled nations and planted it.
10You cleared a place for it;
  it took deep root and filled the land.
11The mountains were covered by its shade,
  mighty cedars by its boughs.
12Its branches reached the sea,
  its shoots, the river.
13Why did You breach its wall
  so that every passerby plucks its fruit,

¹⁴wild boars gnaw at it,
and creatures of the field feed on it?

¹⁵O God of hosts, turn again,
look down from heaven and see;
take note of that vine,
¹⁶the stock planted by Your right hand,
the stem^a you have taken as Your own.
¹⁷For it is burned by fire and cut down,
perishing before Your angry blast.
¹⁸Grant Your help^b to the man at Your right hand,
the one You have taken as Your own.
¹⁹We will not turn away from You;
preserve our life that we may invoke Your name.
²⁰O LORD, God of hosts, restore us;
show Your favor that we may be delivered.

81 For the leader; on the *gittith*. Of Asaph.

²Sing joyously to God, our strength;
raise a shout for the God of Jacob.
³Take up the song,
sound the timbrel,
the melodious lyre and harp.
⁴Blow the horn on the new moon,
on the full moon for our feast day.
⁵For it is a law for Israel,
a ruling of the God of Jacob;
⁶He imposed it as a decree upon Joseph
when ^{a-}he went forth from^{-a} the land of Egypt;
I heard a language that I knew not.

⁷I relieved his shoulder of the burden,
his hands were freed from the basket.
⁸In distress you called and I rescued you;
I answered you from the ^{b-}secret place of thunder^{-b}
I tested you at the waters of Meribah.   *Selah.*

---

^a *Lit. "son."*
^b *Lit. "hand."*

^{a-a} *Or "He went forth against."*
^{b-b} *Meaning of Heb. uncertain.*

97

⁹Hear, My people, and I will admonish you;
　　Israel, if you would but listen to Me!
¹⁰You shall have no foreign god,
　　you shall not bow to an alien god.
¹¹I the LORD am your God
　　who brought you out of the land of Egypt;
　　open your mouth wide and I will fill it.

¹²But My people would not listen to Me,
　　Israel would not obey Me.
¹³So I let them go after their willful heart
　　that they might follow their own devices.
¹⁴If only My people would listen to Me,
　　if Israel would follow My paths,
¹⁵then would I subdue their enemies at once,
　　strike their foes again and again.
¹⁶Those who hate the LORD shall cower before Him;
　　their doom shall be eternal.
¹⁷He fed them^c the finest wheat;
　　I sated you with honey from the rock.

82 A psalm of Asaph.

God stands in the divine assembly;
　　among the divine beings He pronounces judgment.
²How long will you judge perversely,
　　showing favor to the wicked?　　　　　　　　　*Selah.*
³Judge the wretched and the orphan,
　　vindicate the lowly and the poor,
　　⁴rescue the wretched and the needy;
　　save them from the hand of the wicked.

⁵They neither know nor understand,
　　they go about in darkness;
　　all the foundations of the earth totter.
⁶I had taken you for divine beings,
　　sons of the Most High; all of you;

---

^c Lit. *"him,"* i.e., Israel.

7but you shall die as men do,
fall like any prince.

8Arise, O God, judge the earth,
for all the nations are Your possession.

83 A song, a psalm of Asaph.

2O God, do not be silent;
do not hold aloof;
do not be quiet, O God!
3For Your enemies rage,
Your foes a-assert themselves.-a
4They plot craftily against Your people,
take counsel against Your treasured ones.
5They say, "Let us wipe them out as a nation;
Israel's name will be mentioned no more."
6Unanimous in their counsel
they have made an alliance against You—
7the clans of Edom and the Ishmaelites,
Moab and the Hagrites,
8Gebal, Ammon, and Amalek,
Philistia with the inhabitants of Tyre;
9Assyria too joins forces with them;
they give support to the sons of Lot.   *Selah.*

10Deal with them as You did with Midian,
with Sisera, with Jabin,
at the brook Kishon—
11who were destroyed at En-dor,
who became dung for the field.
12Treat their great men like Oreb and Zeeb,
all their princes like Zebah and Zalmunna,
13who said, "Let us take the meadows of God
as our possession."
14O my God, make them like thistledown,
like stubble driven by the wind.

a-a Lit. "lift up the head."

¹⁵As a fire burns a forest,
    as flames scorch the hills,
        ¹⁶pursue them with Your tempest,
    terrify them with Your storm.
¹⁷Cover^b their faces with shame
    so that they seek Your name, O LORD.
¹⁸May they be frustrated and terrified,
    disgraced and doomed forever.
¹⁹May they know
    that Your name, Yours alone, is the LORD,
    supreme over all the earth.

84 For the leader; on the *gittith*. Of the Korahites. A psalm.

²How lovely is Your dwelling-place,
    O LORD of hosts.
³I long, I yearn for the courts of the LORD;
    my body and soul shout for joy to the living God.
⁴Even the sparrow has found a home,
    and the swallow a nest for herself
    in which to set her young,
    near Your altar, O LORD of hosts,
    my king and my God.
⁵Happy are those who dwell in Your house;
    they forever praise You.   *Selah.*

⁶Happy is the man who finds refuge in You,
    whose mind is on the [pilgrim] highways.
⁷They pass through the Valley of Baca,
    ^{a-}regarding it as a place of springs,
    as if the early rain had covered it with blessing.^{-a}
⁸They go from ^{b-}rampart to rampart,^{-b}
    appearing before God in Zion.
⁹O LORD, God of hosts,
    hear my prayer;
    give ear, O God of Jacob.   *Selah.*

^b *Lit. "Fill."*
^{a-a} *Meaning of Heb. uncertain.*
^{b-b} *Others "strength to strength."*

10O God, behold our shield,
  look upon the face of Your anointed.

11Better one day in Your courts than a thousand [anywhere
    else];
  I would rather stand at the threshold of God's house
    than dwell in the tents of the wicked.
12For the LORD God is sunc and shield;
  the LORD bestows grace and glory;
  He does not withhold His bounty from those who live
    without blame.
13O LORD of hosts,
  happy is the man who trusts in You.

85 For the leader. Of the Korahites. A psalm.

2O LORD, You a-will favor-a Your land,
  restoreb Jacob's fortune;
  3You c-will forgive-c Your people's iniquity,
  pardond all their sins;   Selah.
  4You e-will withdraw-e all Your anger,
  turnf away from Your rage.
5Turn again, O God, our helper,
  revoke Your displeasure with us.
6Will You be angry with us forever,
  prolong Your wrath for all generations?
7Surely You will revive us again,
  so that Your people may rejoice in You.
8Show us, O LORD, Your faithfulness;
  grant us Your deliverance.

9Let me hear what God, the LORD, will speak;
  He will promise well-being to His people, His faithful ones;
  may they not turn to folly.
10His help is very near those who fear Him,
  to make His glory dwell in our land.

c Or "bulwark," with Targum; cf. Isa. 54.12.

a-a Or "have favored."
b Or "have restored."
c-c Or "have forgiven."
d Or "have pardoned."
e-e Or "have withdrawn."
f Or "have turned."

¹¹Faithfulness and truth meet;
 justice and well-being kiss.
¹²Truth springs up from the earth;
 justice looks down from heaven.
¹³The LORD also bestows His bounty;
 our land yields its produce.
¹⁴Justice goes before Him
 as He sets out on His way.

86 A prayer of David.

Incline Your ear, O LORD,
 answer me,
 for I am poor and needy.
²Preserve my life, for I am steadfast;
 O You, my God,
 deliver Your servant who trusts in You.
³Have mercy on me, O LORD,
 for I call to You all day long;
⁴bring joy to Your servant's life,
 for on You, LORD, I set my hope.
⁵For You, LORD, are good and forgiving,
 abounding in steadfast love to all who call on You.
⁶Give ear, O LORD, to my prayer;
 heed my plea for mercy.
⁷In my time of trouble I call You,
 for You will answer me.

⁸There is none like You among the gods, O LORD,
 and there are no deeds like Yours.
⁹All the nations You have made
 will come to bow down before You, O LORD,
 and they will pay honor to Your name.
¹⁰For You are great and perform wonders;
 You alone are God.

11Teach me Your way, O LORD;
    I will walk in Your truth;
    let my heart be undivided in reverence for Your name.
12I will praise You, O LORD, my God, with all my heart
    and pay honor to Your name forever.
13For Your steadfast love toward me is great;
    You have saved me from the depths of Sheol.

14O God, arrogant men have risen against me;
    a band of ruthless men seek my life;
    they are not mindful of You.
15But You, O LORD, are a God
    compassionate and merciful,
    slow to anger, abounding in steadfast love and faithfulness.
16Turn to me and have mercy on me;
    grant Your strength to Your servant
    and deliver the son of Your maidservant.
17Show me a sign of Your favor,
    that my enemies may see and be frustrated
    because You, O LORD, have given me aid and comfort.

87 a1-2Of the Korahites. A psalm. A song.

b-The LORD loves the gates of Zion,
    His foundation on the holy mountains,-b
    more than all the dwellings of Jacob.
3Glorious things are spoken of you,
    O city of God.   Selah.
4I mention Rahabc and Babylon among those who acknowledge
        Me;
    Philistia, and Tyre, and Cush—each was born there.
5Indeed, it shall be said of Zion,
    "Every man was born there."
d-He, the Most High, will preserve it.-d
6The LORD will inscribe in the register of peoples
    that each was born there.   Selah.

a The meaning of many passages in this psalm is uncertain.
b-b Order of lines inverted for clarity.
c A primeval monster; here, a poetic term for Egypt; cf. Isa. 30.7.
d-d Or "He will preserve it supreme."

103

⁷Singers and dancers alike [will say]:
"All my roots^c are in You."

88

A song. A psalm of the Korahites. For the leader; ^{a}-on *mahalath leannoth*.$^{-a}$ A *maskil* of Heman the Ezrahite.

²O LORD, God of my deliverance,
^{b}-when I cry out in the night-^{b} before You,
³let my prayer reach You;
incline Your ear to my cry.
⁴For I am sated with misfortune;
I am at the brink of Sheol.
⁵I am numbered with those who go down to the Pit;
I am a helpless man
⁶abandoned^c among the dead,
like bodies lying in the grave
of whom You are mindful no more,
and who are cut off from Your care.
⁷You have put me at the bottom of the Pit,
in the darkest places, in the depths.
⁸Your fury lies heavy upon me;
You afflict me with all Your breakers.   *Selah.*
⁹You make my companions shun me;
You make me abhorrent to them;
I am shut in and do not go out.
¹⁰My eyes pine away from affliction;
I call to You, O LORD, each day;
I stretch out my hands to You.

¹¹Do You work wonders for the dead?
Do the shades rise to praise You?   *Selah.*
¹²Is Your faithful care recounted in the grave,
Your constancy in the place of perdition?
¹³Are Your wonders made known in the netherworld,^{d}
Your beneficent deeds in the land of oblivion?

¹⁴As for me, I cry out to You, O LORD;
each morning my prayer greets You.

---

c Lit. "sources."

a-a Meaning of Heb. uncertain.
b-b Or "by day I cry out [and] by night."
c Lit. "released."
d Lit. "darkness."

15Why, O LORD, do You reject me,
do You hide Your face from me?
16From my youth I have been afflicted
and near death;
I suffer Your terrors e-wherever I turn.-e
17Your fury overwhelms me;
Your terrors destroy me.
18They swirl about me like water all day long;
they encircle me on every side.
19You have put friend and neighbor far from me
and my companions out of my sight.f

89 A *maskil* of Ethan the Ezrahite.

2I will sing of the LORD's steadfast love forever;
to all generations I will proclaim Your faithfulness with my
mouth.
3I declare, "Your steadfast love is confirmed forever;
there in the heavens You establish Your faithfulness."

4"I have made a covenant with My chosen one;
I have sworn to My servant David:
5I will establish your offspring forever,
I will confirm your throne for all generations."   *Selah.*

6Your wonders, O LORD, are praised by the heavens,
Your faithfulness, too, in the assembly of holy beings.
7For who in the skies can equal the LORD,
can compare with the LORD among the divine beings,
8a God greatly dreaded in the council of holy beings,
held in awe by all around Him?
9O LORD, God of hosts,
who is mighty like You, O LORD?
Your faithfulness surrounds You;
10You rule the swelling of the sea;
when its waves surge, You still them.
11You crushed Rahab; he was like a corpse;
with Your powerful arm You scattered Your enemies.
12The heaven is Yours,

e-e *Following Saadia; meaning of Heb. uncertain.*
f *Lit. "into darkness."*

the earth too;
the world and all it holds—
You established them.
¹³North and south—
You created them;
Tabor and Hermon sing forth Your name.
¹⁴Yours is an arm endowed with might;
Your hand is strong;
Your right hand, exalted.
¹⁵Righteousness and justice are the base of Your throne;
steadfast love and faithfulness stand before You.

¹⁶Happy is the people who know the joyful shout;
O LORD, they walk in the light of Your presence.
¹⁷They rejoice in Your name all day long;
they are exalted through Your righteousness.
¹⁸For You are their strength in which they glory;
our horn is exalted through Your favor.
¹⁹Truly our shield is of the LORD,
our king, of the Holy One of Israel.

²⁰Then^a You spoke to Your faithful ones in a vision
and said, "I have conferred power upon a warrior;
I have exalted one chosen out of the people.
²¹I have found David, My servant;
anointed him with My sacred oil.
²²My hand shall be constantly with him,
and My arm shall strengthen him.
²³No enemy shall ᵇ⁻oppress him,⁻ᵇ
no vile man afflict him.
²⁴I will crush his adversaries before him;
I will strike down those who hate him.
²⁵My faithfulness and steadfast love shall be with him;
his horn shall be exalted through My name.
²⁶I will set his hand upon the sea,
his right hand upon the rivers.
²⁷He shall say to Me,

ᵃ *Referring to vv. 4–5; cf. 2 Sam. 7.1–17.*
ᵇ⁻ᵇ *Meaning of Heb. uncertain.*

'You are my father, my God, the rock of my deliverance.'

28I will appoint him first-born,
   highest of the kings of the earth.
29I will maintain My steadfast love for him always;
   My covenant with him shall endure.
30I will establish his line forever,
   his throne, as long as the heavens last.
31If his sons forsake My Teaching
   and do not live by My rules;
   32if they violate My laws,
   and do not observe My commands,
   33I will punish their transgression with the rod,
   their iniquity with plagues.
34But I will not take away My steadfast love from him;
   I will not betray My faithfulness.
35I will not violate My covenant,
   or change what I have uttered.
36I have sworn by My holiness, once and for all;
   I will not be false to David.
37His line shall continue forever,
   his throne, as the sun before Me,
   38as the moon, established forever,
   an enduring witness in the sky."   *Selah.*

39Yet You have rejected, spurned,
   and become enraged at Your anointed.
40You have repudiated the covenant with Your servant;
   You have dragged his dignity in the dust.
41You have breached all his defenses,
   shattered his strongholds.
42All who pass by plunder him;
   he has become the butt of his neighbors.
43You have exalted the right hand of his adversaries,
   and made all his enemies rejoice.
44You have turned back the blade of his sword,
   and have not sustained him in battle.
45You have brought b-his splendor-b to an end

and have hurled his throne to the ground.

⁴⁶You have cut short the days of his youth;
   You have covered him with shame.   *Selah.*

⁴⁷How long, O LORD; will You forever hide Your face,
   will Your fury blaze like fire?

⁴⁸O remember ᵇ⁻how short my life is;⁻ᵇ
   why should You have created every man in vain?

⁴⁹What man can live and not see death,
   can save himself from the clutches of Sheol?   *Selah.*

⁵⁰O LORD, where is Your steadfast love of old
   which You swore to David in Your faithfulness?

⁵¹Remember, O LORD, the abuse flung at Your servants
   ᵇ⁻that I have borne in my bosom [from] many peoples,⁻ᵇ

⁵²how Your enemies, O LORD, have flung abuse,
   abuse at Your anointed at every step.

⁵³Blessed is the LORD forever;
   Amen and Amen.

BOOK FOUR

90 A prayer of Moses, the man of God.

O Lord, You have been our refuge in every generation.

²Before the mountains came into being,
   before You brought forth the earth and the world,
   from eternity to eternity You are God.

³You return man to dust;ᵃ
   You decreed, "Return you mortals!"

⁴ᵇ⁻For in Your sight a thousand years
   are like yesterday that has past,
   like a watch of the night.

⁵You engulf men in sleep;⁻ᵇ
   at daybreak they are like grass that renews itself;

⁶at daybreak it flourishes anew;

ᵃ *Or "contrition."*
ᵇ⁻ᵇ *Meaning of Heb. uncertain.*

by dusk it withers and dries up.
⁷So we are consumed by Your anger,
terror-struck by Your fury.
⁸You have set our iniquities before You,
our hidden sins in the light of Your face.
⁹All our days pass away in Your wrath;
we spend our years like a sigh.
¹⁰The span of our life is seventy years,
or, given the strength, eighty years;
but the ᵇ-best of them-ᵇ are trouble and sorrow.
They pass by speedily, and we ᶜ-are in darkness.-ᶜ
¹¹Who can know Your furious anger?
Your wrath matches the fear of You.
¹²Teach us to count our days rightly,
that we may obtain a wise heart.

¹³Turn, O LORD!
How long?
Show mercy to Your servants.
¹⁴Satisfy us at daybreak with Your steadfast love
that we may sing for joy all our days.
¹⁵Give us joy for as long as You have afflicted us,
for the years we have suffered misfortune.
¹⁶Let Your deeds be seen by Your servants,
Your glory by their children.
¹⁷May the favor of the LORD, our God, be upon us;
let the work of our hands prosper,
O prosper the work of our hands!

91 O you who dwell in the shelter of the Most High
and abide in the protection of Shaddai—
²I say of the LORD, my refuge and stronghold,
my God in whom I trust,
³that He will save you from the fowler's trap,
from the destructive plague.
⁴He will cover you with His pinions;
you will find refuge under His wings;

ᶜ⁻ᶜ *Or "fly away."*

His fidelity is an encircling shield.
⁵You need not fear the terror by night,
   or the arrow that flies by day,
      ⁶the plague that stalks in the darkness,
      or the scourge that ravages at noon.
⁷A thousand may fall at your left side,
   ten thousand at your right,
      but it shall not reach you.
⁸You will see it with your eyes,
   you will witness the punishment of the wicked.
⁹Because you took the LORD—my refuge,
   the Most High—as your haven,
      ¹⁰no harm will befall you,
      no disease touch your tent.
¹¹For He will order His angels
   to guard you wherever you go.
¹²They will carry you in their hands
   lest you hurt your foot on a stone.
¹³You will tread on cubs and vipers;
   you will trample lions and asps.

¹⁴"Because he is devoted to Me I will deliver him;
   I will keep him safe, for he knows My name.
¹⁵When he calls on Me, I will answer him;
   I will be with him in distress;
   I will rescue him and make him honored;
      ¹⁶I will let him live to a ripe old age,
      and show him My salvation."

92

A psalm. A song; for the sabbath day.

²It is good to praise the LORD,
   to sing hymns to Your name, O Most High,
³To proclaim Your steadfast love at daybreak,
   Your faithfulness each night
⁴With a ten-stringed harp,
   with voice and lyre together.

⁵You have gladdened me by Your deeds, O LORD;
  I shout for joy at Your handiwork.
⁶How great are Your works, O LORD,
  how very subtleª Your designs!
⁷A brutish man cannot know,
  a fool cannot understand this:
  ⁸though the wicked sprout like grass,
  though all evildoers blossom,
  it is only that they may be destroyed forever.

⁹But You are exalted, O LORD, for all time.

¹⁰Surely, Your enemies, O LORD,
  surely, Your enemies perish;
  all evildoers are scattered.
¹¹You raise my horn high like that of a wild ox;
  I am soaked in freshening oil.
¹²I shall see the defeat of my watchful foes,
  hear of the downfall of the wicked who beset me.
¹³The righteous bloom like a date-palm;
  they thrive like a cedar in Lebanon;
  ¹⁴planted in the house of the LORD,
  they flourish in the courts of our God.
¹⁵In old age they still produce fruit;
  they are full of sap and freshness,
  ¹⁶attesting that the LORD is upright,
  my rock, in whom there is no wrong.

93 The LORD is king,
  He is robed in grandeur;
  the LORD is robed,
  He is girded with strength.
The world stands firm;
  it cannot be shaken.
²Your throne stands firm from of old;
  from eternity You have existed.
³The ocean sounds, O LORD,

ª Or "profound."

the ocean sounds its thunder,
the ocean sounds its pounding.
4Above the thunder of the mighty waters,
more majestic than the breakers of the sea
is the LORD, majestic on high.
5Your decrees are indeed enduring;
holiness befits Your house,
O LORD, for all times.

94

God of retribution, LORD,
God of retribution, appear!
2Rise up, judge of the earth,
give the arrogant their deserts!
3How long shall the wicked, O LORD,
how long shall the wicked exult,
4shall they utter insolent speech,
shall all evildoers vaunt themselves?
5They crush Your people, O LORD,
they afflict Your very own;
6they kill the widow and the stranger;
they murder the fatherless,
7thinking, "The LORD does not see it,
the God of Jacob does not pay heed."

8Take heed, you most brutish people;
fools, when will you get wisdom?
9Shall He who implants the ear not hear,
He who forms the eye not see?
10Shall He who disciplines nations not punish,
He who instructs men in knowledge?
11The LORD knows the designs of men to be futile.

12Happy is the man whom You discipline, O LORD,
the man You instruct in Your teaching,
13to give him tranquillity in times of misfortune,
until a pit be dug for the wicked.
14For the LORD will not forsake His people;

He will not abandon His very own.
15Judgment shall again accord with justice
and all the upright shall rally to it.

16Who will take my part against evil men?
Who will stand up for me against wrongdoers?
17Were not the LORD my help,
   I should soon dwell in silence.
18When I think my foot has given way,
   Your faithfulness, O LORD, supports me.
19When I am filled with cares,
   Your assurance soothes my soul.

20Shall the seat of injustice be Your partner,
   that frames mischief by statute?
21They band together to do away with the righteous;
   they condemn the innocent to death.
22But the LORD is my haven;
   my God is my sheltering rock.
23He will make their evil recoil upon them,
   annihilate them through their own wickedness;
   the LORD our God will annihilate them.

95 Come, let us sing joyously to the LORD,
   raise a shout for our rock and deliverer;
   2let us come into His presence with praise;
   let us raise a shout for Him in song!
3For the LORD is a great God,
   the great king of all divine beings.
4In His hand are the depths of the earth;
   the peaks of the mountains are His.
5His is the sea, He made it;
   and the land, which His hands fashioned.

6Come, let us bow down and kneel,
   bend the knee before the LORD our maker,
   7for He is our God,

and we are the people He tends, the flock in His care.
O, if you would but heed His charge this day:
 8Do not be stubborn as at Meribah,
 as on the day of Massah, in the wilderness,
 9when your fathers put Me to the test,
 tried Me, though they had seen My deeds.
 10Forty years I was provoked by that generation;
I thought, "They are a senseless people;
 they would not know My ways."
 11Concerning them I swore in anger,
 "They shall never come to My resting-place!"

96

 ᵃSing to the LORD a new song,
 sing to the LORD, all the earth.
 2Sing to the LORD, bless His name,
 proclaim His victory day after day.
 3Tell of His glory among the nations,
 His wondrous deeds, among all peoples.
 4For the LORD is great and much acclaimed,
 He is held in awe by all divine beings.
 5All the gods of the peoples are mere idols,
 but the LORD made the heavens.
 6Glory and majesty are before Him;
 strength and splendor are in His temple.

 7Ascribe to the LORD, O families of the peoples,
 ascribe to the LORD glory and strength.
 8Ascribe to the LORD the glory of His name,
 bring tribute and enter His courts.
 9Bow down to the LORD majestic in holiness;
 tremble in His presence, all the earth!
 10Declare among the nations, "The LORD is king!"
 the world stands firm; it cannot be shaken;
 He judges the peoples with equity.
 11Let the heavens rejoice and the earth exult;
 let the sea and all within it thunder,
 12the fields and everything in them exult;

ᵃ *Cf. 1 Chron. 16.23–33.*

then shall all the trees of the forest shout for joy
13at the presence of the LORD, for He is coming,
for He is coming to rule the earth;
He will rule the world justly,
and its peoples in faithfulness.

97

The LORD is king!
Let the earth exult,
the many islands rejoice!
2Dense clouds are around Him,
righteousness and justice are the base of His throne.
3Fire is His vanguard,
burning His foes on every side.
4His lightnings light up the world;
the earth is convulsed at the sight;
5mountains melt like wax at the LORD's presence,
at the presence of the Lord of all the earth.
6The heavens proclaim His righteousness
and all peoples see His glory.
7All who worship images,
who vaunt their idols,
are dismayed;
all divine beings bow down to Him.
8Zion, hearing it, rejoices,
the towns[a] of Judah exult,
because of Your judgments, O LORD.
9For You, LORD, are supreme over all the earth;
You are exalted high above all divine beings.

10O you who love the LORD, hate evil!
He guards the lives of His loyal ones,
saving them from the hand of the wicked.
11Light is sown for the righteous,
radiance[b] for the upright.
12O you righteous, rejoice in the LORD
and acclaim His holy name!

a Or "women."
b Others "joy."

98 A psalm.

Sing to the LORD a new song,
  for He has worked wonders;
  His right hand, His holy arm,
  has won Him victory.
²The LORD has manifested His victory,
  has displayed His triumph in the sight of the nations.
³He was mindful of His steadfast love and faithfulness
    toward the house of Israel;
  all the ends of the earth beheld the victory of our God.
⁴Raise a shout to the LORD, all the earth,
  break into joyous songs of praise!
⁵Sing praise to the LORD with the lyre,
  with the lyre and melodious song.
⁶With trumpets and the blast of the horn
  raise a shout before the LORD, the king.
⁷Let the sea and all within it thunder,
  the world and its inhabitants;
  ⁸let the rivers clap their hands,
  the mountains sing joyously together
  ⁹at the presence of the LORD,
  for He is coming to rule the earth;
  He will rule the world justly,
  and its peoples with equity.

99 ᵃ⁻The LORD, enthroned on cherubim, is king,
  peoples tremble, the earth quakes.⁻ᵃ
²The LORD is great in Zion,
  and exalted above all peoples.
³They praise Your name as great and awesome;
  He is holy!

⁴ᵇ⁻Mighty king⁻ᵇ who loves justice,
  it was You who established equity,

ᵃ⁻ᵃ *Clauses transposed for clarity.*
ᵇ⁻ᵇ *Meaning of Heb. uncertain.*

You who worked righteous judgment in Jacob.
⁵Exalt the LORD our God
and bow down to His footstool;
He is holy!

⁶Moses and Aaron among His priests,
Samuel, among those who call on His name—
when they called to the LORD,
He answered them.
⁷He spoke to them in a pillar of cloud;
they obeyed His decrees,
the law He gave them.
⁸O LORD our God, You answered them;
You were a forgiving God for them,
but You exacted retribution for their misdeeds.

⁹Exalt the LORD our God,
and bow toward His holy hill,
for the LORD our God is holy.

100 A psalm ᵃ⁻for praise.⁻ᵃ

Raise a shout for the LORD, all the earth;
²worship the LORD in gladness;
come into His presence with shouts of joy.
³Acknowledge that the LORD is God;
He made us and ᵇ⁻we are His,⁻ᵇ
His people, the flock He tends.
⁴Enter His gates with praise,
His courts with acclamation.
Praise Him!
Bless His name!
⁵For the LORD is good;
His steadfast love is eternal;
His faithfulness is for all generations.

ᵃ⁻ᵃ *Traditionally "for the thanksgiving offering."*
ᵇ⁻ᵇ *So* qere; kethib *and some ancient versions "not we ourselves."*

101 Of David. A psalm.

I will sing of faithfulness and justice;
  I will chant a hymn to You, O Lord.
[2]I will study the way of the blameless;
  when shall I attain it?
I will live without blame within my house.
[3]I will not set before my eyes anything base;
  I hate crooked dealing;
  I will have none of it.
[4]Perverse thoughts will be far from me;
  I will know nothing of evil.
[5]He who slanders his friend in secret I will destroy;
  I cannot endure the haughty and proud man.
[6]My eyes are on the trusty men of the land,
  to have them at my side.
He who follows the way of the blameless
  shall be in my service.
[7]He who deals deceitfully
  shall not live in my house;
  he who speaks untruth
  shall not stand before my eyes.
[8]Each morning I will destroy
  all the wicked of the land,
  to rid the city of the Lord
  of all evildoers.

102 A prayer of the lowly man when he is faint and pours forth his plea before the Lord.

[2]O Lord, hear my prayer;
  let my cry come before You.
[3]Do not hide Your face from me
  in my time of trouble;
  turn Your ear to me;
  when I cry, answer me speedily.

⁴For my days have vanished like smoke
   and my bones are charred like a hearth.
⁵My body is stricken and withered like grass;
     ᵃ⁻too wasted⁻ᵃ to eat my food;
       ⁶on account of my vehement groaning
       my bones ᵇ⁻show through my skin.⁻ᵇ
⁷I am like a great owl in the wilderness,
   an owl among the ruins.
⁸I lie awake; I am like
   a lone bird upon a roof.
⁹All day long my enemies revile me;
   my deriders use my name to curse.
¹⁰For I have eaten ashes like bread
   and mixed my drink with tears,
     ¹¹because of Your wrath and Your fury;
     for You have cast me far away.
¹²My days are like a lengthening shadow;
   I wither like grass.

¹³But You, O LORD, are enthroned forever;
   Your fame endures throughout the ages.
¹⁴You will surely arise and take pity on Zion,
   for it is time to be gracious to her;
   the appointed time has come.
¹⁵Your servants take delight in its stones,
   and cherish its dust.
¹⁶The nations will fear the name of the LORD,
   all the kings of the earth, Your glory.
¹⁷For the LORD has built Zion;
   He has appeared in all His glory.
¹⁸He has turned to the prayer ᶜ⁻of the destitute⁻ᶜ
   and has not spurned their prayer.
¹⁹May this be written down for a coming generation,
   that people yet to be created may praise the LORD.
²⁰For He looks down from His holy height;
   the LORD beholds the earth from heaven
     ²¹to hear the groans of the prisoner,
     to release those condemned to death;

ᵃ⁻ᵃ Others "I forget."
ᵇ⁻ᵇ Lit. "cling to my flesh."
ᶜ⁻ᶜ Meaning of Heb. uncertain.

²²that the fame of the LORD may be recounted in Zion,
His praises in Jerusalem,
²³when the nations gather together,
the kingdoms, to serve the LORD.

²⁴He drained my strength in mid-course,
He shortened my days.
²⁵I say, "O my God, do not take me away
in the midst of my days,
You whose years go on for generations on end.
²⁶Of old You established the earth;
the heavens are the work of Your hands.
²⁷They shall perish, but You shall endure;
they shall all wear out like a garment;
You change them like clothing and they pass away.
²⁸But You are the same, and Your years never end.
²⁹May the children of Your servants dwell securely
and their offspring endure in Your presence."

103 Of David.

Bless the LORD, O my soul,
all my being, His holy name.
²Bless the LORD, O my soul
and do not forget all His bounties.
³He forgives all your sins,
heals all your diseases.
⁴He redeems your life from the Pit,
surrounds you with steadfast love and mercy.
⁵He satisfies you with good things in ª·the prime of life,·ª
so that your youth is renewed like the eagle's.

⁶The LORD executes righteous acts
and judgments for all who are wronged.
⁷He made known His ways to Moses,
His deeds to the children of Israel.
⁸The LORD is compassionate and gracious,

ª·ª *Meaning of Heb. uncertain.*

120

slow to anger, abounding in steadfast love.
⁹He will not contend forever,
  or nurse His anger for all time.
¹⁰He has not dealt with us according to our sins,
  nor has He requited us according to our iniquities.
¹¹For as the heavens are high above the earth,
  so great is His steadfast love toward those who fear Him.
¹²As east is far from west,
  so far has He removed our sins from us.
¹³As a father has compassion for his children,
  so the LORD has compassion for those who fear Him.
¹⁴For He knows how we are formed;
  He is mindful that we are dust.

¹⁵Man, his days are like those of grass;
  he blooms like a flower of the field;
    ¹⁶a wind passes by and it is no more,
    its own place no longer knows it.
¹⁷But the LORD's steadfast love is for all eternity
  toward those who fear Him,
  and His beneficence is for the children's children
    ¹⁸of those who keep His covenant
  and remember to observe His precepts.
¹⁹The LORD has established His throne in heaven,
  and His sovereign rule is over all.

²⁰Bless the LORD, O His angels,
  mighty creatures who do His bidding,
  ever obedient to His bidding;
    ²¹bless the LORD, all His hosts,
  His servants who do His will;
    ²²bless the LORD, all His works,
  through the length and breadth of His realm;
  bless the LORD, O my soul.

104

Bless the LORD, O my soul;
  O LORD, my God, You are very great;

You are clothed in glory and majesty,
²wrapped in a robe of light;
You spread the heavens like a tent cloth.
³He sets the rafters of His lofts in the waters,
makes the clouds His chariot,
moves on the wings of the wind.
⁴He makes the winds His messengers,
fiery flames His servants.
⁵He established the earth on its foundations,
so that it shall never totter.
⁶You made the deep cover it as a garment;
the waters stood above the mountains.
⁷They fled at Your blast,
rushed away at the sound of Your thunder,
⁸—mountains rising, valleys sinking—
to the place You established for them.
⁹You set bounds they must not pass
so that they never again cover the earth.

¹⁰You make springs gush forth in torrents;
they make their way between the hills,
¹¹giving drink to all the wild beasts;
the wild asses slake their thirst.
¹²The birds of the sky dwell beside them
and sing among the foliage.
¹³You water the mountains from Yourᵃ lofts;
the earth is sated from the fruit of Your work.
¹⁴You make the grass grow for the cattle,
and herbage for man's labor
that he may get food out of the earth—
¹⁵wine that cheers the hearts of men
ᵇ‑oil that makes the face shine,‑ᵇ
and bread that sustains man's life.
¹⁶The trees of the LORD drink their fill,
the cedars of Lebanon, His own planting,
¹⁷where birds make their nests;
the stork has her home in the junipers.

ᵃ *Lit. "His."*
ᵇ⁻ᵇ *Lit. "to make the face shine from oil."*

122

18The high mountains are for wild goats;
   the crags are a refuge for rock-badgers.

19He made the moon to mark the seasons;
   the sun knows when to set.
20You bring on darkness and it is night,
   when all the beasts of the forests stir.
21The lions roar for prey,
   seeking their food from God.
22When the sun rises, they come home
   and couch in their dens.
23Man then goes out to his work,
   to his labor until the evening.

24How many are the things You have made, O LORD;
   You have made them all with wisdom;
   the earth is full of Your creations.
25There is the sea, vast and wide,
   with its creatures beyond number,
   living things, small and great.
26There go the ships,
   and Leviathan that You formed to sport with.
27All of them look to You
   to give them their food when it is due.
28Give it to them, they gather it up;
   open Your hand, they are well satisfied;
   29hide Your face, they are terrified;
   take away their breath, they perish
   and turn again into dust;
   30send back Your breath, they are created,
   and You renew the face of the earth.

31May the glory of the LORD endure forever;
   may the LORD rejoice in His works!
32He looks at the earth and it trembles;
   He touches the mountains and they smoke.

³³I will sing to the LORD as long as I live;
  all my life I will chant hymns to my God.
³⁴May my prayer be pleasing to Him;
  I will rejoice in the LORD.
³⁵May sinners disappear from the earth,
  and the wicked be no more.
Bless the LORD, O my soul.
  Hallelujah.

105

Praise the LORD;
  call on His name;
  proclaim His deeds among the peoples.
²Sing praises to Him;
  speak of all His wondrous acts.
³Exult in His holy name;
  let all who seek the LORD rejoice.
⁴Turn to the LORD, to His might;^a
  seek His presence constantly.
⁵Remember the wonders He has done,
  His portents and the judgments He has pronounced,
⁶O offspring of Abraham, His servant,
  O descendants of Jacob, His chosen ones.

⁷He is the LORD our God;
  His judgments are throughout the earth.
⁸He is ever mindful of His covenant,
  the promise He gave for a thousand generations,
⁹that He made with Abraham,
swore to Isaac,
¹⁰and confirmed in a decree for Jacob,
for Israel, as an eternal covenant,
¹¹saying, "To you I will give the land of Canaan
as your allotted heritage."

¹²They were then few in number,
  a mere handful, sojourning there,
¹³wandering from nation to nation,

---

^a *I.e., the Ark; cf. Ps. 78.61; 132.8.*

from one kingdom to another.

14He allowed no one to oppress them;
He reproved kings on their account,
15"Do not touch My anointed ones;
do not harm My prophets."

16He called down a famine on the land,
destroyed every staff of bread.
17He sent ahead of them a man,
Joseph, sold into slavery.
18His feet were subjected to fetters;
an iron collar was put on his neck.
19Until his prediction came true
the decree of the LORD purged him.
20The king sent to have him freed;
the ruler of nations released him.
21He made him the lord of his household,
empowered him over all his possessions,
22to discipline his princes at will,
to teach his elders wisdom.
23Then Israel came to Egypt;
Jacob sojourned in the land of Ham.

24He made His people very fruitful,
more numerous than their foes.
25b-He changed their heart-b to hate His people,
to plot against His servants.
26He sent His servant Moses,
and Aaron, whom He had chosen.
27They performed His signs among them,
His wonders, against the land of Ham.
28He sent darkness; it was very dark;
c-did they not defy His word?-c
29He turned their waters into blood
and killed their fish.
30Their land teemed with frogs,
even the rooms of their king.
31Swarms of insects came at His command,

b-b Or "Their heart changed."
c-c Meaning of Heb. uncertain.

lice, throughout their country.
³²He gave them hail for rain,
  and flaming fire in their land.
³³He struck their vines and fig trees,
  broke down the trees of their country.
³⁴Locusts came at His command,
  grasshoppers without number.
³⁵They devoured every green thing in the land;
  they consumed the produce of the soil.
³⁶He struck down every first-born in the land,
  the first fruit of their vigor.
³⁷He led Israelᵈ out with silver and gold;
  none among their tribes faltered.
³⁸Egypt rejoiced when they left,
  for dread of Israelᵈ had fallen upon them.

³⁹He spread a cloud for a cover,
  and fire to light up the night.
⁴⁰They asked and He brought them quail,
  and satisfied them with food from heaven.
⁴¹He opened a rock so that water gushed forth;
  it flowed as a stream in the parched land.
⁴²Mindful of His sacred promise
  to His servant Abraham,
⁴³He led His people out in gladness,
  His chosen ones with joyous song.
⁴⁴He gave them the lands of nations;
  they inherited the wealth of peoples,
⁴⁵that they might keep His laws
  and observe His teachings.
  Hallelujah.

106 Hallelujah.

Praise the LORD for He is good;
  His steadfast love is eternal.

ᵈ Lit. "them."

126

²Who can tell the mighty acts of the LORD,
   proclaim all His praises?

³Happy are those who act justly,
   who do right at all times.
⁴Be mindful of me, O LORD, when You favor Your people;
   take note of me when You deliver them,
   ⁵that I may enjoy the prosperity of Your chosen ones,
   share the joy of Your nation,
   glory in Your very own people.

⁶We have sinned like our forefathers;
   we have gone astray, done evil.
⁷Our forefathers in Egypt did not perceive Your wonders;
   they did not remember Your abundant love,
   but rebelled at the sea, at the Sea of Reeds.
⁸Yet He saved them, as befits His name,
   to make known His might.
⁹He sent His blast against the Sea of Reeds;
   it became dry;
   He led them through the deep as through a wilderness.
¹⁰He delivered them from the foe,
   redeemed them from the enemy.
¹¹Water covered their adversaries;
   not one of them was left.
¹²Then they believed His promise,
   and sang His praises.
¹³But they soon forgot His deeds;
   they would not wait to learn His plan.
¹⁴They were seized with craving in the wilderness,
   and put God to the test in the wasteland.
¹⁵He gave them what they asked for,
   then made them waste away.
¹⁶There was envy of Moses in the camp,
   and of Aaron, the holy one of the LORD.
¹⁷The earth opened up and swallowed Dathan,
   closed over the party of Abiram.

¹⁸A fire blazed among their party,
   a flame that consumed the wicked.
¹⁹They made a calf at Horeb
   and bowed down to a molten image.
²⁰They exchanged their glory
   for the image of a bull that feeds on grass.
²¹They forgot God who saved them,
   who performed great deeds in Egypt,
²²wondrous deeds in the land of Ham,
   awesome deeds at the Sea of Reeds.
²³He would have destroyed them
   had not Moses His chosen one
   confronted Him in the breach
   to avert His destructive wrath.
²⁴They rejected the desirable land,
   and put no faith in His promise.
²⁵They grumbled in their tents
   and disobeyed the LORD.
²⁶So He raised His hand in oath
   to make them fall in the wilderness,
²⁷to disperse[a] their offspring among the nations
   and scatter them through the lands.
²⁸They attached themselves to Baal Peor,
   ate sacrifices offered to the dead.
²⁹They provoked anger by their deeds,
   and a plague broke out among them.
³⁰Phinehas stepped forth and intervened,
   and the plague ceased.
³¹It was reckoned to his merit
   for all generations, to eternity.
³²They provoked wrath at the waters of Meribah
   and Moses suffered on their account,
³³because they rebelled against Him
   and he spoke rashly.

³⁴They did not destroy the nations
   as the LORD had commanded them,

ᵃ Cf. Targum, Kimhi.

³⁵but mingled with the nations
and learned their ways.
³⁶They worshiped their idols,
which became a snare for them.
³⁷Their own sons and daughters
they sacrificed to demons.
³⁸They shed innocent blood,
the blood of their sons and daughters,
whom they sacrificed to the idols of Canaan;
so the land was polluted with bloodguilt.
³⁹Thus they became defiled by their acts,
debauched through their deeds.
⁴⁰The LORD was angry with His people
and He abhorred His inheritance.
⁴¹He handed them over to the nations;
their foes ruled them.
⁴²Their enemies oppressed them
and they were subject to their power.
⁴³He saved them time and again,
but they were deliberately rebellious,
and so they were brought low by their iniquity.
⁴⁴When He saw that they were in distress,
when He heard their cry,
⁴⁵He was mindful of His covenant
and in His great faithfulness relented.
⁴⁶He made all their captors kindly disposed toward them.

⁴⁷Deliver us, O LORD our God,
and gather us from among the nations,
to acclaim Your holy name,
to glory in Your praise.

⁴⁸Blessed is the LORD, God of Israel,
From eternity to eternity.
Let all the people say, "Amen."
Hallelujah.

BOOK FIVE

107 "Praise the LORD, for He is good;
His steadfast love is eternal!"
²Thus let the redeemed of the LORD say,
those He redeemed from adversity,
³whom He gathered in from the lands,
from east and west,
from the north and from the sea.

⁴Some lost their way in the wilderness,
in the wasteland;
they found no settled place.
⁵Hungry and thirsty,
their spirit failed.
⁶In their adversity they cried to the LORD,
and He rescued them from their troubles.
⁷He showed them a direct way
to reach a settled place.
⁸Let them praise the LORD for His steadfast love,
His wondrous deeds for mankind;
⁹for He has satisfied the thirsty,
filled the hungry with all good things.

¹⁰Some lived in deepest darkness,
bound in cruel irons,
¹¹because they defied the word of God,
spurned the counsel of the Most High.
¹²He humbled their hearts through suffering;
they stumbled with no one to help.
¹³In their adversity they cried to the LORD,
and He rescued them from their troubles.
¹⁴He brought them out of deepest darkness,
broke their bonds asunder.
¹⁵Let them praise the LORD for His steadfast love,
His wondrous deeds for mankind,
¹⁶For He shattered gates of bronze,
He broke their iron bars.

17There were fools who suffered for their sinful way,
and for their iniquities.
18All food was loathsome to them;
they reached the gates of death.
19In their adversity they cried to the LORD
and He saved them from their troubles.
20He gave an order and healed them;
He delivered them from the pits.ᵃ
21Let them praise the LORD for His steadfast love,
His wondrous deeds for mankind.
22Let them offer thanksgiving sacrifices,
and tell His deeds in joyful song.

23Others go down to the sea in ships,
ply their trade in the mighty waters;
24they have seen the works of the LORD
and His wonders in the deep.
25By His word He raised a storm wind
that made the waves surge.
26Mounting up to the heaven,
plunging down to the depths,
disgorging in their misery,
27they reeled and staggered like a drunken man,
all their skill to no avail.
28In their adversity they cried to the LORD,
and He saved them from their troubles.
29He reduced the storm to a whisper;
the waves were stilled.
30They rejoiced when all was quiet,
and He brought them to the port they desired.
31Let them praise the LORD for His steadfast love,
His wondrous deeds for mankind.
32Let them exalt Him in the congregation of the people,
acclaim Him in the assembly of the elders.

33He turns the rivers into a wilderness,
springs of water into thirsty land,
34fruitful land into a salt marsh,
because of the wickedness of its inhabitants.

ᵃ Viz., of death.

³⁵He turns the wilderness into pools,
    parched land into springs of water.
³⁶There He settles the hungry;
    they build a place to settle in.
³⁷They sow fields and plant vineyards
    that yield a fruitful harvest.
³⁸He blesses them and they increase greatly;
    and He does not let their cattle decrease,
³⁹after they had been few and crushed
    by oppression, misery, and sorrow.
⁴⁰He pours contempt on great men
    and makes them lose their way in trackless deserts;
⁴¹but the needy He secures from suffering,
    and increases their families like flocks.

⁴²The upright see it and rejoice;
    the mouth of all wrongdoers is stopped.
⁴³The wise man will take note of these things;
    he will consider the steadfast love of the LORD.

108 A song. A psalm of David.

²ᵃMy heart is firm, O God;
    I will sing and chant a hymn with all my soul.
³Awake, O harp and lyre!
    I will wake the dawn.
⁴I will praise You among the peoples, O LORD,
    sing a hymn to You among the nations;
⁵for Your faithfulness is higher than the heavens;
    Your steadfastness reaches to the sky.
⁶Exalt Yourself over the heavens, O God;
    let Your glory be over all the earth!
⁷ᵇThat those whom You love may be rescued,
    deliver with Your right hand and answer me.

⁸God promised ᶜ⁻in His sanctuary⁻ᶜ
    that I would exultingly divide up Shechem,

ᵃ *With vv. 2–6, cf. Ps. 57.8–12.*
ᵇ *With vv. 7–14, cf. Ps. 60.7–14.*
ᶜ⁻ᶜ *Or "by His holiness."*

132

and measure the Valley of Sukkoth;
⁹Gilead and Manasseh would be mine,
Ephraim my chief stronghold,
Judah my scepter;
¹⁰Moab would be my washbasin;
on Edom I would cast my shoe;
I would raise a shout over Philistia.
¹¹Would that I were brought to the bastion!
Would that I were led to Edom!

¹²But You have rejected us, O God;
God, You do not march with our armies.
¹³Grant us Your aid against the foe,
for the help of man is worthless.
¹⁴With God we shall triumph;
He will trample our foes.

109 For the leader. Of David. A psalm.

O God of my praise,
do not keep aloof,
²for the wicked and the deceitful
open their mouth against me;
they speak to me with lying tongue.
³They encircle me with words of hate;
they attack me without cause.
⁴They answer my love with accusation
ᵃ⁻and I must stand judgment.⁻ᵃ
⁵They repay me with evil for good,
with hatred for my love.

⁶Appoint a wicked man over him;
may an accuser stand at his right side;
⁷may he be tried and convicted;
may he be judged and found guilty.
⁸May his days be few;
may another take over ᵇ⁻his position.⁻ᵇ

ᵃ⁻ᵃ Or "but I am all prayer"; meaning of Heb. uncertain, but see v. 7.
ᵇ⁻ᵇ Meaning of Heb. uncertain.

⁹May his children be orphans,
  his wife a widow.
¹⁰May his children wander from their hovels,
  begging in search of [bread].
¹¹May his creditor seize all his possessions;
  may strangers plunder his wealth.
¹²May no one show him mercy;
  may none pity his orphans;
    ¹³may his posterity be cut off;
  may their names be blotted out in the next generation.
¹⁴May God be ever mindful of his father's iniquity,
  and may the sin of his mother not be blotted out.
¹⁵May the LORD be aware of them always
  and cause their names to be cut off from the earth,
    ¹⁶because he was not minded to act kindly,
  and hounded to death the poor and needy man,
  one crushed in spirit.
¹⁷He loved to curse—may a curse come upon him!
He would not bless—may blessing be far from him!
¹⁸May he be clothed in a curse like a garment,
  may it enter his body like water,
  his bones like oil.
¹⁹Let it be like the cloak he wraps around him,
  like the belt he always wears.
²⁰May the LORD thus repay my accusers,
  all those who speak evil against me.

²¹Now You, O God, my Lord,
  act on my behalf as befits Your name.
Good and faithful as You are, save me.
²²For I am poor and needy,
  and my heart is pierced within me.
²³I fade away like a lengthening shadow;
  I am shaken off like locusts.
²⁴My knees give way from fasting;
  my flesh is lean, has lost its fat.
²⁵I am the object of their scorn;
  when they see me, they shake their head.

26Help me, O LORD, my God;
    save me in accord with Your faithfulness,
    27that men may know that it is Your hand,
    that You, O LORD, have done it.
28Let them curse, but You bless;
    let them rise up, but come to grief,
    while Your servant rejoices.
29My accusers shall be clothed in shame,
    wrapped in their disgrace as in a robe.

30My mouth shall sing much praise to the LORD;
    I will acclaim Him in the midst of a throng,
    31because He stands at the right hand of the needy,
    to save him from those who would condemn him.

110 Of David. A psalm.

The LORD said to my lord,
    "Sit at My right hand
    while I make your enemies your footstool."

2The LORD will stretch forth from Zion your mighty scepter;
    hold sway over your enemies!
3a·Your people come forward willingly on your day of battle.
In majestic holiness, from the womb,
    from the dawn, yours was the dew of youth.·a

4The LORD has sworn and will not relent,
    "You are a priest forever, b·a rightful king by My decree."·b
5The Lord is at your right hand.
He crushes kings in the day of His anger.

6He works judgment upon the nations,
    heaping up bodies,
    crushing heads far and wide.
7He drinks from the stream on his way;
    therefore he holds his head high.

a-a *Meaning of Heb. uncertain.*
b-b *Or "after the manner of Melchizedek."*

111 Hallelujah.

א I praise the LORD with all my heart
ב   in the assembled congregation of the upright.
ג ²The works of the LORD are great,
ד   a-within reach of all who desire them.-a
ה ³His deeds are splendid and glorious;
ו   His beneficence is everlasting;
ז   ⁴He has won renown for His wonders.
ח The LORD is gracious and compassionate;
ט   ⁵He gives food to those who fear Him;
י   He is ever mindful of His covenant.
כ ⁶He revealed to His people His powerful works,
ל   in giving them the heritage of nations.
מ ⁷His handiwork is truth and justice;
נ   all His precepts are enduring,
ס   ⁸well-founded for all eternity,
ע   wrought of truth and equity.
פ ⁹He sent redemption to His people;
צ   He ordained His covenant for all time;
ק   His name is holy and awesome.
ר ¹⁰The beginningᵇ of wisdom is the fear of the LORD;
ש   all who practice it gain sound understanding.
ת Praise of Him is everlasting.

112 Hallelujah.

א Happy is the man who fears the LORD,
ב   who is ardently devoted to His commandments.
ג ²His descendants will be mighty in the land,
ד   a blessed generation of upright men.
ה ³Wealth and riches are in his house,
ו   and his beneficence lasts forever.
ז ⁴a-A light shines-a for the upright in the darkness;
ח   he is gracious, compassionate, and beneficent.
ט ⁵All goes well with the man who lends generously,
י   who conducts his affairs with equity.
כ ⁶He shall never be shaken;

---

a-a Meaning of Heb. uncertain.
ᵇ Or "chief part."
a-a Or "He shines as a light."

ל   the beneficent man will be remembered forever.

מ   7He is not afraid of evil tidings;

נ   his heart is firm, he trusts in the LORD.

ס   8His heart is resolute, he is unafraid;

ע   in the end he will see the fall of his foes.

פ   9He gives freely to the poor;

צ   his beneficence lasts forever;

ק   his horn is exalted in honor.

ר   10The wicked man shall see it and be vexed;

ש   he shall gnash his teeth; his courage shall fail.

ת   The desire of the wicked shall come to nothing.

113
Hallelujah.
O servants of the LORD, give praise;
    praise the name of the LORD.
2Let the name of the LORD be blessed
    now and forever.
3From east to west
    the name of the LORD is praised.
4The LORD is exalted above all nations;
    His glory is above the heavens.
5Who is like the LORD our God,
    who, enthroned on high,
      6sees what is below,
    in heaven and on earth?
7He raises the poor from the dust,
    lifts up the needy from the refuse heap
      8to set them with the great,
    with the great men of His people.
9He sets the childless woman among her household
    as a happy mother of children.
    Hallelujah.

114
When Israel went forth from Egypt,
    the house of Jacob from a people of strange speech,
    2Judah became His a-holy one,-a

---

a-a Or "sanctuary."

Israel, His dominion.
³The sea saw them and fled,
Jordan ran backward,
⁴mountains skipped like rams,
hills like sheep.
⁵What alarmed you, O sea, that you fled,
Jordan, that you ran backward,
⁶mountains, that you skipped like rams,
hills, like sheep?
⁷Tremble, O earth, at the presence of the LORD,
at the presence of the God of Jacob,
⁸who turned the rock into a pool of water,
the flinty rock into a fountain.

115 Not to us, O LORD, not to us
but to Your name bring glory
for the sake of Your love and Your faithfulness.
²Let the nations not say,
"Where, now, is their God?"
³when our God is in heaven
and all that He wills He accomplishes.
⁴ᵃTheir idols are silver and gold,
the work of men's hands.
⁵They have mouths, but cannot speak,
eyes, but cannot see;
⁶they have ears, but cannot hear,
noses, but cannot smell;
⁷they have hands, but cannot touch,
feet, but cannot walk;
they can make no sound in their throats.
⁸Those who fashion them,
all who trust in them,
shall become like them.
⁹O Israel, trust in the LORD!
He is their help and shield.
¹⁰O house of Aaron, trust in the LORD!
He is their help and shield.

ᵃ *With vv. 4–11, cf. Ps. 135.15–20.*

¹¹O you who fear the LORD, trust in the LORD!
He is their help and shield.

¹²The LORD is mindful of us.
He will bless us;
    He will bless the house of Israel;
    He will bless the house of Aaron;
    ¹³He will bless those who fear the LORD,
    small and great alike.

¹⁴May the LORD increase your numbers,
    yours and your children's also.
¹⁵May you be blessed by the LORD,
    Maker of heaven and earth.
¹⁶The heavens belong to the LORD,
    but the earth He gave over to man.
¹⁷The dead cannot praise the LORD,
    nor any who go down into silence.
¹⁸But we will bless the LORD
    now and forever.
    Hallelujah.

116

ᵃ·I love the LORD
    for He hears·ᵃ my voice, my pleas;
    ²for He turns His ear to me
    whenever I call.
³The bonds of death encompassed me;
    the torments of Sheol overtook me.
I came upon trouble and sorrow
    ⁴and I invoked the name of the LORD,
    "O LORD, save my life!"

⁵The LORD is gracious and beneficent;
    our God is compassionate.
⁶The LORD protects the simple;
    I was brought low and He saved me.
⁷Be at rest, once again, O my soul,

ᵃ⁻ᵃ *Heb. transposed for clarity; others "I would love that the LORD hear," etc.*

for the LORD has been good to you.
8You[b] have delivered me from death,
my eyes from tears,
my feet from stumbling.
9I shall walk before the LORD
in the lands of the living.
10c-I trust [in the LORD];
out of great suffering I spoke-c
11and said rashly,
"All men are false."

12How can I repay the LORD
for all His bounties to me?
13I raise the cup of deliverance
and invoke the name of the LORD.
14I will pay my vows to the LORD
in the presence of all His people.
15The death of His faithful ones
is grievous in the LORD's sight.

16O LORD,
I am Your servant,
Your servant, the son of Your maidservant;
You have undone the cords that bound me.
17I will sacrifice a thank offering to You
and invoke the name of the LORD.
18I will pay my vows to the LORD
in the presence of all His people,
19in the courts of the house of the LORD,
in the midst of[d] Jerusalem.
Hallelujah.

117

Praise the LORD, all you nations;
extol Him, all you peoples,
2for great is His steadfast love toward us;
the faithfulness of the LORD endures forever.
Hallelujah.

b *I.e., God.*
c-c *Meaning of Heb. uncertain.*
d *Others "of you."*

118 Praise the LORD, for He is good,
His steadfast love is eternal.
²Let Israel declare,
"His steadfast love is eternal."
³Let the house of Aaron declare,
"His steadfast love is eternal."
⁴Let those who fear the LORD declare,
"His steadfast love is eternal."

⁵In distress I called on the LORD;
the Lord answered me and brought me relief.
⁶The LORD is on my side,
I have no fear;
what can man do to me?
⁷With the LORD on my side as my helper,
I will see the downfall of my foes.

⁸It is better to take refuge in the LORD
than to trust in mortals;
⁹it is better to take refuge in the LORD
than to trust in the great.

¹⁰All nations have beset me;
by the name of the LORD I will surely ᵃ⁻cut them down.⁻ᵃ
¹¹They beset me, they surround me;
by the name of the LORD I will surely cut them down.
¹²They have beset me like bees;
they shall be extinguished like burning thorns;
by the name of the LORD I will surely cut them down.

¹³Youᵇ pressed me hard,
I nearly fell;
but the LORD helped me.
¹⁴The LORD is my strength and might;ᶜ
He has become my deliverance.
¹⁵The tents of the victoriousᵈ resound with joyous shouts of
deliverance,

ᵃ⁻ᵃ *Meaning of 'amilam in this and the following two verses uncertain.*
ᵇ *I.e., the enemy.*
ᶜ *Others "song."*
ᵈ *Or "righteous."*

"The right hand of the LORD is triumphant!
16The right hand of the LORD is exalted!
The right hand of the LORD is triumphant!"

17I shall not die but live
   and proclaim the works of the LORD.
18The LORD punished me severely,
   but did not hand me over to death.

19Open the gates of victory^c for me
   that I may enter them and praise the LORD.
20This is the gateway to the LORD—
   the victorious^d shall enter through it.

21I praise You, for You have answered me,
   and have become my deliverance.
22The stone that the builders rejected
   has become the chief cornerstone.
23This is the LORD's doing;
   it is marvelous in our sight.
24This is the day that the LORD has made—
   let us exult and rejoice on it.

25O LORD, deliver us!
O LORD, let us prosper!

26May he who enters be blessed in the name of the LORD;
   we bless you from the House of the LORD.
27The LORD is God;
   He has given us light;
   f-bind the festal offering to the horns of the altar with cords.-f
28You are my God and I will praise You;
   You are my God and I will extol You.
29Praise the LORD for He is good,
   His steadfast love is eternal.

c Or "righteousness."
f-f Meaning of Heb. uncertain.

119

א Happy are those whose way is blameless,
who follow the teaching of the LORD.
²Happy are those who observe His decrees,
who turn to Him wholeheartedly.
³They have done no wrong,
but have followed His ways.
⁴You have commanded that Your precepts
be kept diligently.
⁵Would that my ways were firm
in keeping Your laws;
⁶then I would not be ashamed
when I regard all Your commandments.
⁷I will praise You with a sincere heart
as I learn Your just rules.
⁸I will keep Your laws;
do not utterly forsake me.

ב ⁹How can a young man keep his way pure?—
by holding to Your word.
¹⁰I have turned to You with all my heart;
do not let me stray from Your commandments.
¹¹In my heart I treasure Your promise;
therefore I do not sin against You.
¹²Blessed are You, O LORD;
train me in Your laws.
¹³With my lips I rehearse
all the rules You proclaimed.
¹⁴I rejoice over the way of Your decrees
as over all riches.
¹⁵I study Your precepts;
I regard Your ways;
¹⁶I take delight in Your laws;
I will not neglect Your word.

ג ¹⁷Deal kindly with Your servant,
that I may live to keep Your word.

¹⁸Open my eyes, that I may perceive
the wonders of Your teaching.
¹⁹I am only a sojourner in the land;
do not hide Your commandments from me.
²⁰My soul is consumed with longing
for Your rules at all times.
²¹You blast the accursed insolent ones
who stray from Your commandments.
²²Take away from me taunt and abuse,
because I observe Your decrees.
²³Though princes meet and speak against me,
Your servant studies Your laws.
²⁴For Your decrees are my delight,
my intimate companions.

ד

²⁵My soul clings to the dust;
revive me in accordance with Your word.
²⁶I have declared my way, and You have answered me;
train me in Your laws.
²⁷Make me understand the way of Your precepts,
that I may study Your wondrous acts.
²⁸I am racked with grief;
sustain me in accordance with Your word.
²⁹Remove all false ways from me;
favor me with Your teaching.
³⁰I have chosen the way of faithfulness;
I have set Your rules before me.
³¹I cling to Your decrees;
O LORD, do not put me to shame.
³²I eagerly pursue Your commandments,
for You broaden my understanding.

ה

³³Teach me, O LORD, the way of Your laws;
I will observe them ^{a-}to the utmost.^{-a}
³⁴Give me understanding, that I may observe Your teaching
and keep it wholeheartedly.
³⁵Lead me in the path of Your commandments,
for that is my concern.

^{a-a} *Meaning of Heb. uncertain.*

³⁶Turn my heart to Your decrees
and not to love of gain.
³⁷Avert my eyes from seeing falsehood;
by Your ways preserve me.
³⁸Fulfill Your promise to Your servant,
which is for those who worship You.
³⁹Remove the taunt that I dread,
for Your rules are good.
⁴⁰See, I have longed for Your precepts;
by Your righteousness preserve me.

ו ⁴¹May Your steadfast love reach me, O LORD,
Your deliverance, as You have promised.
⁴²I shall have an answer for those who taunt me,
for I have put my trust in Your word.
⁴³Do not utterly take the truth away from my mouth,
for I have put my hope in Your rules.
⁴⁴I will always obey Your teaching,
forever and ever.
⁴⁵I will walk about at ease,
for I have turned to Your precepts.
⁴⁶I will speak of Your decrees,
and not be ashamed in the presence of kings.
⁴⁷I will delight in Your commandments,
which I love.
⁴⁸I reach out for Your commandments, which I love;
I study Your laws.

ז ⁴⁹Remember Your word to Your servant
through which You have given me hope.
⁵⁰This is my comfort in my affliction,
that Your promise has preserved me.
⁵¹Though the arrogant have cruelly mocked me,
I have not swerved from Your teaching.
⁵²I remember Your rules of old, O LORD,
and find comfort in them.
⁵³I am seized with rage
because of the wicked who forsake Your teaching.

⁵⁴Your laws are ᵇ⁻a source of strength to me⁻ᵇ
    wherever I may dwell.
⁵⁵I remember Your name at night, O LORD,
    and obey Your teaching.
⁵⁶This has been my lot,
    for I have observed Your precepts.

ח ⁵⁷The LORD is my portion;
    I have resolved to keep Your words.
⁵⁸I have implored You with all my heart;
    have mercy on me, in accordance with Your promise.
⁵⁹I have considered my ways,
    and have turned back to Your decrees.
⁶⁰I have hurried and not delayed
    to keep Your commandments.
⁶¹Though the bonds of the wicked are coiled round me,
    I have not neglected Your teaching.
⁶²I arise at midnight to praise You
    for Your just rules.
⁶³I am a companion to all who fear You,
    to those who keep Your precepts.
⁶⁴Your steadfast love, O LORD, fills the earth;
    teach me Your laws.

ט ⁶⁵You have treated Your servant well,
    according to Your word, O LORD.
⁶⁶Teach me good sense and knowledge,
    for I have put my trust in Your commandments.
⁶⁷Before I was humbled I went astray,
    but now I keep Your word.
⁶⁸You are good and beneficent;
    teach me Your laws.
⁶⁹Though the arrogant have accused me falsely,
    I observe Your precepts wholeheartedly.
⁷⁰Their minds are thick like fat;
    as for me, Your teaching is my delight.
⁷¹It was good for me that I was humbled,

ᵇ⁻ᵇ Or *"songs for me."*

so that I might learn Your laws.

72I prefer the teaching You proclaimed
    to thousands of gold and silver pieces.

י 73Your hands made me and fashioned me;
    give me understanding that I may learn Your
      commandments.

74Those who fear You will see me and rejoice,
    for I have put my hope in Your word.

75I know, O LORD, that Your rulings are just;
    rightly have You humbled me.

76May Your steadfast love comfort me
    in accordance with Your promise to Your servant.

77May Your mercy reach me, that I might live,
    for Your teaching is my delight.

78Let the insolent be dismayed, for they have
    wronged me without cause;
    I will study Your precepts.

79May those who fear You,
    those who know Your decrees,
    turn again to me.

80May I wholeheartedly follow Your laws
    so that I do not come to grief.

כ 81I long for Your deliverance;
    I hope for Your word.

82My eyes pine away for Your promise;
    I say, "When will You comfort me?"

83Though I have become like a water-skin dried in smoke,
    I have not neglected Your laws.

84How long has Your servant to live?
    when will You bring my persecutors to judgment?

85The insolent have dug pits for me,
    flouting Your teaching.

86All Your commandments are enduring;
    I am persecuted without cause; help me!

87Though they almost wiped me off the earth,

I did not abandon Your precepts.
88As befits Your steadfast love, preserve me,
so that I may keep the decree You proclaimed.

ל 89The LORD exists forever;
Your word stands firm in heaven.
90Your faithfulness is for all generations;
You have established the earth, and it stands.
91They stand this day to [carry out] Your rulings,
for all are Your servants.
92Were not Your teaching my delight
I would have perished in my affliction.
93I will never neglect Your precepts,
for You have preserved my life through them.
94I am Yours; save me!
For I have turned to Your precepts.
95The wicked hope to destroy me,
but I ponder Your decrees.
96I have seen that all things have their limit,
but Your commandment is broad beyond measure.

מ 97O how I love Your teaching!
It is my study all day long.
98Your commandments make me wiser than my enemies;
they always stand by me.
99I have gained more insight than all my teachers,
for Your decrees are my study.
100I have gained more understanding than my elders,
for I observe Your precepts.
101I have avoided every evil way
so that I may keep Your word.
102I have not departed from Your rules,
for You have instructed me.
103How pleasing is Your word to my palate,
sweeter than honey.
104I ponder Your precepts;
therefore I hate every false way.

ל 105Your word is a lamp to my feet,
a light for my path.
106I have firmly sworn
to keep Your just rules.
107I am very much afflicted;
O LORD, preserve me in accordance with Your word.
108Accept, O LORD, my freewill offerings;
teach me Your rules.
109Though my life is always in danger,
I do not neglect Your teaching.
110Though the wicked have set a trap for me,
I have not strayed from Your precepts.
111Your decrees are my eternal heritage;
they are my heart's delight.
112I am resolved to follow Your laws
a-to the utmost-a forever.

מ 113I hate men of divided heart,
but I love Your teaching.
114You are my protection and my shield;
I hope for Your word.
115Keep away from me, you evildoers,
that I may observe the commandments of my God.
116Support me as You promised, so that I may live;
do not thwart my expectation.
117Sustain me that I may be saved,
and I will always muse upon Your laws.
118You reject all who stray from Your laws,
for they are false and deceitful.
119You do away with the wicked as if they were dross;
rightly do I love Your decrees.
120My flesh creeps from fear of You;
I am in awe of Your rulings.

ע 121I have done what is just and right;
do not abandon me to those who would wrong me.
122Guarantee Your servant's well-being;
do not let the arrogant wrong me.

123My eyes pine away for Your deliverance,
    for Your promise of victory.
124Deal with Your servant as befits Your steadfast love;
    teach me Your laws.
125I am Your servant;
    give me understanding,
    that I might know Your decrees.
126It is a time to act for the LORD,
    for they have violated Your teaching.
127Rightly do I love Your commandments
    more than gold, even fine gold.
128Truly c-by all [Your] precepts I walk straight;-c
    I hate every false way.

פ   129Your decrees are wondrous;
    rightly do I observe them.
130d-The words You inscribed give-d light,
    and grant understanding to the simple.
131I open my mouth wide, I pant,
    longing for Your commandments.
132Turn to me and be gracious to me,
    as is Your rule with those who love Your name.
133Make my feet firm through Your promise;
    do not let iniquity dominate me.
134Redeem me from being wronged by man,
    that I may keep Your precepts.
135Show favor to Your servant,
    and teach me Your laws.
136My eyes shed streams of water
    because men do not obey Your teaching.

צ   137You are righteous, O LORD;
    Your rulings are just.
138You have ordained righteous decrees;
    they are firmly enduring.
139I am consumed with rage
    over my foes' neglect of Your words.
140Your word is exceedingly pure,

c-c *Or "I declare all [Your] precepts to be just."*
d-d *With Targum; or "The exposition of Your words gives"; meaning of Heb. uncertain.*

and Your servant loves it.

141Though I am belittled and despised,
   I have not neglected Your precepts.
142Your righteousness is eternal;
   Your teaching is true.
143Though anguish and distress come upon me,
   Your commandments are my delight.
144Your righteous decrees are eternal;
   give me understanding, that I might live.

ק 145I call with all my heart;
   answer me, O LORD,
   that I may observe Your laws.
146I call upon You; save me,
   that I may keep Your decrees.
147I rise before dawn and cry for help;
   I hope for Your word.
148My eyes greet each watch of the night,
   as I meditate on Your promise.
149Hear my voice as befits Your steadfast love;
   O LORD, preserve me, as is Your rule.
150Those who pursue intrigue draw near;
   they are far from Your teaching.
151You, O LORD, are near,
   and all Your commandments are true.
152I know from Your decrees of old
   that You have established them forever.

ר 153See my affliction and rescue me,
   for I have not neglected Your teaching.
154Champion my cause and redeem me;
   preserve me according to Your promise.
155Deliverance is far from the wicked,
   for they have not turned to Your laws.
156Your mercies are great, O LORD;
   as is Your rule, preserve me.
157Many are my persecutors and foes;
   I have not swerved from Your decrees.

¹⁵⁸I have seen traitors and loathed^c them,
because they did not keep Your word in mind.
¹⁵⁹See that I have loved Your precepts;
O LORD, preserve me, as befits Your steadfast love.
¹⁶⁰Truth is the essence of Your word;
Your just rules are eternal.

ש   ¹⁶¹Princes have persecuted me without reason;
my heart thrills at Your word.
¹⁶²I rejoice over Your promise
as one who obtains great spoil.
¹⁶³I hate and abhor falsehood;
I love Your teaching.
¹⁶⁴I praise You seven times each day
for Your just rules.
¹⁶⁵Those who love Your teaching enjoy well-being;
they encounter no adversity.
¹⁶⁶I hope for Your deliverance, O LORD;
I observe Your commandments.
¹⁶⁷I obey Your decrees
and love them greatly.
¹⁶⁸I obey Your precepts and decrees;
all my ways are before You.

ת   ¹⁶⁹May my plea reach You, O LORD;
grant me understanding according to Your word.
¹⁷⁰May my petition come before You;
save me in accordance with Your promise.
¹⁷¹My lips shall pour forth praise,
for You teach me Your laws.
¹⁷²My tongue shall declare Your promise,
for all Your commandments are just.
¹⁷³Lend Your hand to help me,
for I have chosen Your precepts.
¹⁷⁴I have longed for Your deliverance, O LORD;
Your teaching is my delight.
¹⁷⁵Let me live, that I may praise You;
may Your rules be my help;

---

c *Or "have contended with."*

176I have strayed like a lost sheep;
    search for Your servant,
      for I have not neglected Your commandments.

120 A song of ascents.ᵃ

In my distress I called to the LORD
    and He answered me.
2O LORD, save me from treacherous lips,
    from a deceitful tongue!
3What can you profit,
    what can you gain,
    O deceitful tongue?
4A warrior's sharp arrows,
    with hot coals of broom-wood.

5Woe is me, that I live with Meshech,
    that I dwell among the clans of Kedar.
6Too long have I dwelt with those who hate peace.
7I am all peace;
    but when I speak,
    they are for war.

121 A song for ascents.

I turn my eyes to the mountains;
    from where will my help come?
2My help comes from the LORD,
    maker of heaven and earth.
3He will not let your foot give way;
    your guardian will not slumber;
4See, the guardian of Israel
    neither slumbers nor sleeps!
5The LORD is your guardian,
    the LORD is your protection
    at your right hand.

ᵃ *A term of uncertain meaning.*

⁶By day the sun will not strike you,
  nor the moon by night.
⁷The LORD will guard you from all harm;
  He will guard your life.
⁸The LORD will guard your going and coming
  now and forever.

122 A song of ascents. Of David.

I rejoiced when they said to me,
  "We are going to the House of the LORD."
²Our feet stood inside your gates, O Jerusalem,
³Jerusalem built up, a city knit together,
⁴to which tribes would make pilgrimage,
  the tribes of the LORD,
  —as was enjoined upon Israel—
  to praise the name of the LORD.
⁵There the thrones of judgment stood,
  thrones of the house of David.
⁶Pray for the well-being of Jerusalem;
  "May those who love you be at peace.
⁷May there be well-being within your ramparts,
  peace in your citadels."
⁸For the sake of my kin and friends,
  I pray for your well-being;
⁹for the sake of the house of the LORD our God,
  I seek your good.

123 A song of ascents.

To You, enthroned in heaven,
  I turn my eyes.
²As the eyes of slaves follow their master's hand,
  as the eyes of a slave-girl follow the hand of her mistress,
  so our eyes are toward the LORD our God,
  awaiting His favor.

3Show us favor, O LORD,
    show us favor!
We have had more than enough of contempt.
4Long enough have we endured
    the scorn of the complacent,
    the contempt of the haughty.

124 A song of ascents. Of David.

Were it not for the LORD, who was on our side,
    let Israel now declare,
    2were it not for the LORD, who was on our side
    when men assailed us,
    3they would have swallowed us alive
    in their burning rage against us;
    4the waters would have carried us off,
    the torrent would have swept over us;
    5over us would have swept
    the seething waters.
6Blessed is the LORD, who did not let us
    be ripped apart by their teeth.
7We are like a bird escaped from the fowler's trap;
    the trap broke and we escaped.
8Our help is the name of the LORD,
    maker of heaven and earth.

125 A song of ascents.

Those who trust in the LORD
    are like Mount Zion
    that cannot be moved,
    enduring forever.
2Jerusalem, hills enfold it,
    and the LORD enfolds His people
    now and forever.
        3a·The scepter of the wicked shall never rest

a-a *Meaning of Heb. uncertain.*

155

upon the land allotted to the righteous,
that the righteous not set their hand to wrongdoing.[-a]
4Do good, O LORD, to the good,
to the upright in heart.
5a-But those who in their crookedness act corruptly,[-a]
let the LORD make them go the way of evildoers.
May it be well with Israel!

126 A song of ascents.

When the LORD restores the fortunes of Zion
—[a-]we see it as in a dream[-a]—
2our mouths shall be filled with laughter,
our tongues, with songs of joy.
Then shall they say among the nations,
"The LORD has done great things for them!"
3The LORD will do great things for us
and we shall rejoice.

4Restore our fortunes, O LORD,
like watercourses in the Negeb.
5They who sow in tears
shall reap with songs of joy.
6Though he goes along weeping,
carrying the seed-bag,
he shall come back with songs of joy,
carrying his sheaves.

127 A song of ascents. Of Solomon.

Unless the LORD builds the house,
its builders labor in vain on it;
unless the LORD watches over the city,
the watchman keeps vigil in vain.
2In vain do you rise early

---

a-a Lit. "we are veritable dreamers."

and stay up late,
you who toil for the bread you eat;
a·He provides as much for His loved ones while they sleep.·a

3Sons are the provisionb of the LORD;
the fruit of the womb, His reward.
4Like arrows in the hand of a warrior
are sons born to a man in his youth.
5Happy is the man who fills his quiver with them;
they shall not be put to shame
when they contend with the enemy in the gate.

128 A song of ascents.

Happy are all who fear the LORD,
who follow His ways.
2You shall enjoy the fruit of your labors;
you shall be happy and you shall prosper.
3Your wife shall be like a fruitful vine within your house;
your sons, like olive saplings around your table.
4So shall the man who fears the LORD be blessed.

5May the LORD bless you from Zion;
may you share the prosperity of Jerusalem
all the days of your life,
6and live to see your children's children.
May all be well with Israel!

129 A song of ascents.

Since my youth they have often assailed me,
let Israel now declare,
2since my youth they have often assailed me,
but they have never overcome me.
3Plowmen plowed across my back;

a·a Meaning of Heb. uncertain.
b Lit. "heritage."

they made long furrows.
⁴The LORD, the righteous one,
    has snapped the cords of the wicked.

⁵Let all who hate Zion
    fall back in disgrace.
⁶Let them be like grass on roofs
    that fades before it can be pulled up,
      ⁷that affords no handful for the reaper,
    no armful for the gatherer of sheaves,
    ⁸no exchange with passersby:
    "The blessing of the LORD be upon you."
"We bless you by the name of the LORD."

130 A song of ascents.

Out of the depths I call You, O LORD.
²O Lord, listen to my cry;
    let Your ears be attentive
    to my plea for mercy.
³If You keep account of sins, O LORD,
    Lord, who will survive?
⁴Yours is the power to forgive
    so that You may be held in awe.

⁵I look to the LORD;
    I look to Him;
    I await His word.
⁶I am more eager for the Lord
    than watchmen for the morning,
    watchmen for the morning.

⁷O Israel, wait for the LORD;
    for with the LORD is steadfast love
    and great power to redeem.
⁸It is He who will redeem Israel from all their iniquities.

131 A song of ascents. Of David.

O LORD, my heart is not proud
   nor my look haughty;
I do not aspire to great things
   or to what is beyond me;
2a-but I have taught myself to be contented
   like a weaned child with its mother;
   like a weaned child am I in my mind.-a
3O Israel, wait for the LORD
   now and forever.

132 A song of ascents.

O LORD, remember in David's favor
   his extreme self-denial,
2how he swore to the LORD,
   vowed to the Mighty One of Jacob,
3"I will not enter my house,
   nor will I mount my bed,
4I will not give sleep to my eyes,
   or slumber to my eyelidsa
5until I find a place for the LORD,
   an abode for the Mighty One of Jacob."

6We heard it was in Ephrath;
   we came upon it in the region of Jaar.b
7Let us enter His abode,
   bow at His footstool.
8Advance, O LORD, to Your resting-place,
   You and Your mighty Ark!
9Your priests are clothed in triumph;
   Your loyal ones sing for joy.
10For the sake of Your servant David
   do not reject Your anointed one.

---

a-a *Meaning of Heb. uncertain.*
a *Lit. "eyes."*
b *Cf. 1 Sam. 7.1–2; 1 Chron. 13.5–6.*

11The LORD swore to David
    a firm oath that He will not renounce,
    "One of your own issue I will set your throne.
12If your sons keep My covenant
    and My decrees that I teach them,
    then their sons also,
    to the end of time,
    shall sit upon your throne."
13For the LORD has chosen Zion;
    He has desired it for His seat.
14"This is my resting-place for all time;
    here I will dwell, for I desire it.
15I will amply bless its store of food,
    give its needy their fill of bread.
16I will clothe its priests in victory,
    its loyal ones shall sing for joy.
17There I will make a horn sprout for David;
    I have prepared a lamp for My anointed one.
18I will clothe his enemies in disgrace,
    while on him his crown shall sparkle."

133 A song of ascents. Of David.

How good and how pleasant it is
    that brothers dwell together.
2It is like fine oil on the head
    running down onto the beard,
    the beard of Aaron,
    that comes down over the collar of his robe;
3like the dew of Hermon
    that falls upon the mountains of Zion.
There the LORD ordained blessing,
    everlasting life.

134 A song of ascents.

Now bless the LORD,
    all you servants of the LORD
    who stand nightly
    in the house of the LORD.
²Lift your hands toward the sanctuary
    and bless the LORD.
³May the LORD,
    maker of heaven and earth,
    bless you from Zion.

135 Hallelujah.

Praise the name of the LORD;
    give praise, you servants of the LORD
    ²who stand in the house of the LORD,
    in the courts of the house of our God.
³Praise the LORD, for the LORD is good;
    sing hymns to His name, for it is pleasant.
⁴For the LORD has chosen Jacob for Himself,
    Israel, as His treasured possession.

⁵For I know that the LORD is great,
    that our LORD is greater than all gods.
⁶Whatever the LORD desires He does
    in heaven and earth,
    in the seas and all the depths.
⁷He makes clouds rise from the end of the earth;
    He makes lightning for the rain;
    He releases the wind from His vaults.
⁸He struck down the first-born of Egypt,
    man and beast alike;
⁹He sent signs and portents against* Egypt,
    against Pharaoh and all his servants;
¹⁰He struck down many nations
    and slew numerous kings—

---

* Others "against you."

¹¹Sihon, king of the Amorites,
Og, king of Bashan,
and all the royalty of Canaan—
¹²and gave their lands as a heritage,
as a heritage to His people Israel.

¹³O LORD, Your name endures forever,
Your fame, O LORD, through all generations;
¹⁴for the LORD will champion His people,
and obtain satisfaction for His servants.

^{15b}The idols of the nations are silver and gold,
the work of men's hands.
¹⁶They have mouths, but cannot speak;
they have eyes, but cannot see;
¹⁷they have ears, but cannot hear,
nor is there breath in their mouths.
¹⁸Those who fashion them,
all who trust in them,
shall become like them.

¹⁹O house of Israel, bless the LORD;
O house of Aaron, bless the LORD;
²⁰O house of Levi, bless the LORD;
you who fear the LORD, bless the LORD.
²¹Blessed is the LORD from Zion,
He who dwells in Jerusalem.
Hallelujah.

136

Praise the LORD; for He is good,
His steadfast love is eternal.
²Praise the God of gods,
His steadfast love is eternal.
³Praise the Lord of lords,
His steadfast love is eternal;
⁴Who alone works great marvels,
His steadfast love is eternal;

b *With vv. 15–20, cf. Ps. 115.4–11.*

5Who made the heavens with wisdom,
  His steadfast love is eternal;
6Who spread the earth over the water,
  His steadfast love is eternal;
7Who made the great lights,
  His steadfast love is eternal;
8the sun to dominate the day,
  His steadfast love is eternal;
9the moon and the stars to dominate the night,
  His steadfast love is eternal;
10Who struck Egypt through their first-born,
  His steadfast love is eternal;
11and brought Israel out of their midst,
  His steadfast love is eternal;
12with a strong hand and outstretched arm,
  His steadfast love is eternal;
13Who split apart the Sea of Reeds,
  His steadfast love is eternal;
14and made Israel pass through it,
  His steadfast love is eternal;
15Who hurled Pharaoh and his army into the Sea of Reeds,
  His steadfast love is eternal;
16Who led His people through the wilderness,
  His steadfast love is eternal;
17Who struck down great kings,
  His steadfast love is eternal;
18and slew mighty kings—
  His steadfast love is eternal;
19Sihon, king of the Amorites,
  His steadfast love is eternal;
20Og, king of Bashan—
  His steadfast love is eternal;
21and gave their land as a heritage,
  His steadfast love is eternal;
22a heritage to His servant Israel,
  His steadfast love is eternal;
23Who took note of us in our degradation,
  His steadfast love is eternal;

²⁴and rescued us from our enemies,
    His steadfast love is eternal;
²⁵Who gives food to all flesh,
    His steadfast love is eternal.
²⁶Praise the God of heaven,
    His steadfast love is eternal.

137

By the rivers of Babylon,
    there we sat,
    sat and wept,
    as we thought of Zion.
²There on the poplars
    we hung up our lyres,
    ³for our captors asked us there for songs,
    our tormentors,[a] for amusement,
    "Sing us one of the songs of Zion."
⁴How can we sing a song of the LORD
    on alien soil?
⁵If I forget you, O Jerusalem,
    let my right hand wither;[b]
    ⁶let my tongue stick to my palate
    if I cease to think of you,
    if I do not keep Jerusalem in memory
    even at my happiest hour.

⁷Remember, O LORD, against the Edomites
    the day of Jerusalem's fall;
    how they cried, "Strip her, strip her
    to her very foundations!"
⁸Fair Babylon, you predator,[c]
    a blessing on him who repays you in kind
    what you have inflicted on us;
    ⁹a blessing on him who seizes your babies
    and dashes them against the rocks!

[a] *Meaning of Heb. uncertain.*
[b] *Others "forget its cunning."*
[c] *With Targum; others "who are to be destroyed."*

138 Of David.

I praise You with all my heart,
  sing a hymn to You before the divine beings;
²I bow toward Your holy temple
  and praise Your name for Your steadfast love 'and
    faithfulness,
  because You have exalted ᵃ⁻Your name, Your word,
    above all.⁻ᵃ
³When I called, You answered me,
  ᵃ⁻You inspired me with courage.⁻ᵃ
⁴All the kings of the earth shall praise You, O LORD,
  for they have heard the words You spoke.
⁵They shall sing of the ways of the LORD,
  "Great is the majesty of the LORD!"
⁶High though the LORD is, He sees the lowly;
  lofty, He perceives from afar.
⁷Though I walk among enemies,
  You preserve me in the face of my foes;
  You extend Your hand;
  with Your right hand You deliver me.
⁸The LORD will settle accounts for me.
O LORD, Your steadfast love is eternal;
  do not forsake the work of Your hands.

139 For the leader. Of David. A psalm.

O LORD, You have examined me and know me.
²When I sit down or stand up You know it;
  You discern my thoughts from afar.
³ᵃ⁻You observe⁻ᵃ my walking and reclining,
  and are familiar with all my ways.
⁴There is not a word on my tongue
  but that You, O LORD, know it well.
⁵You hedge me before and behind;
  You lay Your hand upon me.

ᵃ⁻ᵃ *Meaning of Heb. uncertain.*
ᵇ⁻ᵇ *Meaning of Heb. uncertain.*

⁶It is beyond my knowledge;
    it is a mystery; I cannot fathom it.
⁷Where can I escape from Your spirit?
Where can I flee from Your presence?
⁸If I ascend to heaven, You are there;
    if I descend to Sheol, You are there too.
⁹If I take wing with the dawn
    to come to rest on the western horizon,
      ¹⁰even there Your hand will be guiding me,
      Your right hand will be holding me fast.
¹¹If I say, "Surely darkness ᵇ⁻will conceal me,
    night will provide me with cover,"⁻ᵇ
      ¹²darkness is not dark for You;
    night is as light as day;
    darkness and light are the same.
¹³It was You who created my conscience;ᶜ
    You fashioned me in my mother's womb.
¹⁴I praise You,
    for I am awesomely, wondrously made;
    Your work is wonderful;
    I know it very well.
¹⁵My frame was not concealed from You
    when I was shaped in a hidden place,
    knit together in the recesses of the earth.
¹⁶Your eyes saw my unformed limbs;
    they were all recorded in Your book;
    in due time they were formed,
    ᵃ⁻to the very last one of them.⁻ᵃ
¹⁷How weighty Your thoughts seem to me, O God,
    how great their number!
¹⁸I count them—they exceed the grains of sand;
    I end—but am still with You.

¹⁹O God, if You would only slay the wicked—
    you murderers, away from me!—
      ²⁰ᵃ⁻who invoke You for intrigue,
    Your enemies who swear by You falsely.⁻ᵃ
²¹O LORD, You know I hate those who hate You,

ᵇ⁻ᵇ *Cf. Rashi, Ibn Ezra; meaning of Heb. uncertain.*
ᶜ *Lit. "kidneys."*

and loathe Your adversaries.
²²I feel a perfect hatred toward them;
   I count them my enemies.

²³Examine me, O God, and know my mind;
   probe me and know my thoughts.
²⁴See if I have vexatious ways,
   and guide me in ways everlasting.

140 For the leader. A psalm of David.

²Rescue me, O LORD, from evil men;
   save me from the lawless,
   ³whose minds are full of evil schemes,
   who plot war every day.
⁴They sharpen their tongues like serpents;
   spiders' poison is on their lips.   *Selah.*

⁵O LORD, keep me out of the clutches of the wicked;
   save me from lawless men
   who scheme to ^{a-}make me fall.^{-a}
⁶Arrogant men laid traps with ropes for me;
   they spread out a net along the way;
   they set snares for me.   *Selah.*

⁷I said to the LORD: You are my God;
   give ear, O LORD, to my pleas for mercy.
⁸O GOD, my Lord, the strength of my deliverance,
   You protected my head on the day of battle.^b
⁹O LORD, do not grant the desires of the wicked;
   do not let their plan succeed,
   ^{c-}else they be exalted.   *Selah.*

¹⁰May the heads of those who beset me
   be covered with the mischief of their lips.^{-c}
¹¹may coals of fire drop down upon them,
   and they be cast into pits, never to rise again.

^{a-a} Lit. *"push my feet."*
^b Lit. *"arms."*
^{c-c} *Meaning of Heb. uncertain.*

¹²Let slanderers have no place in the land;
    let the evil of the lawless man drive him into corrals.
¹³I know that the LORD will champion
    the cause of the poor, the right of the needy.
¹⁴Righteous men shall surely praise Your name;
    the upright shall dwell in Your presence.

141 A psalm of David.

I call You, O LORD, hasten to me;
    give ear to my cry when I call You.
²Take my prayer as an offering of incense,
    my upraised hands as an evening sacrifice.
³O LORD, set a guard over my mouth,
    a watch at the door of my lips;
⁴let my mind not turn to an evil thing,
    to practice deeds of wickedness
    with men who are evildoers;
    let me not feast on their dainties.
⁵ᵃLet the righteous man strike me in loyalty,
    let him reprove me;
    let my head not refuse such choice oil.
My prayers are still against theirᵇ evil deeds.
⁶May their judges slip on the rock,
    but let my words be heard, for they are sweet.
⁷As when the earth is cleft and broken up
    our bones are scattered at the mouth of Sheol.
⁸My eyes are fixed upon You, O GOD my Lord;
    I seek refuge in You, do not put me in jeopardy.
⁹Keep me from the trap laid for me,
    and from the snares of evildoers.
¹⁰Let the wicked fall into their nets
    while I alone come through.

ᵃ *Meaning of vv. 5–7 uncertain.*
ᵇ *I.e., the evildoers of v. 4.*

142

A *maskil* of David, while he was in the cave.[a] A prayer.

[2]I cry aloud to the LORD;
  I appeal to the LORD loudly for mercy.
[3]I pour out my complaint before Him;
  I lay my trouble before Him
    [4]when my spirit fails within me.
You know my course;
  they have laid a trap in the path I walk.
[5]Look at my right and see—
  I have no friend;
  there is nowhere I can flee,
  no one cares about me.
[6]So I cry to You, O LORD;
  I say, "You are my refuge,
  all I have in the land of the living."
[7]Listen to my cry, for I have been brought very low;
  save me from my pursuers,
  for they are too strong for me.
[8]Free me from prison,
  that I may praise Your name.
The righteous [b-]shall glory in me[-b]
  for Your gracious dealings with me.

143

A psalm of David.

O LORD, hear my prayer;
  give ear to my plea, as You are faithful;
  answer me, as You are beneficent.
[2]Do not enter into judgment with Your servant,
  for before You no creature is in the right.

[3]My foe hounded me;
  he crushed me to the ground;
  he made me dwell in darkness
  like those long dead.

a Cf. 1 Sam. 24.3–4.
b-b *Meaning of Heb. uncertain.*

⁴My spirit failed within me;
    my mind was numbed with horror.
⁵Then I thought of the days of old;
    I rehearsed all Your deeds,
    recounted the work of Your hands.
⁶I stretched out my hands to You,
    longing for You like thirsty earth.   *Selah.*

⁷Answer me quickly, O LORD;
    my spirit can endure no more.
Do not hide Your face from me,
    or I shall become like those who descend into the Pit.
⁸Let me learn of Your faithfulness by daybreak,
    for in You I trust;
    let me know the road I must take,
    for on You I have set my hope.
⁹Save me from my foes, O LORD;
    ᵃ⁻to You I look for cover.⁻ᵃ
¹⁰Teach me to do Your will,
    for You are my God.
Let Your gracious spirit lead me
    on level ground.
¹¹For the sake of Your name, O LORD, preserve me;
    as You are beneficent, free me from distress.
¹²As You are faithful, put an end to my foes;
    destroy all my mortal enemies,
    for I am Your servant.

144 Of David.

Blessed is the LORD, my rock,
    who trains my hands for battle,
    my fingers for warfare;
    ²my faithful one, my fortress,
    my haven and my deliverer,
    my shield, in whom I take shelter,

ᵃ⁻ᵃ *Meaning of Heb. uncertain.*

who makes peoples[a] subject to me.

³O LORD, what is man that You should care about him,
   mortal man, that You should think of him?
⁴Man is like a breath;
   his days are like a passing shadow.
⁵O LORD, bend Your sky and come down;
   touch the mountains and they will smoke.
⁶Make lightning flash and scatter them;
   shoot Your arrows and rout them.
⁷Reach Your hand down from on high;
   rescue me, save me from the mighty waters,
   from the hands of foreigners,
   ⁸whose mouths speak lies,
   and whose oaths[b] are false.

⁹O God, I will sing You a new song,
   sing a hymn to You with a ten-stringed harp,
   ¹⁰to You who give victory to kings,
   who rescue His servant David from the deadly sword.
¹¹Rescue me, save me from the hands of foreigners,
   whose mouths speak lies,
   and whose oaths[b] are false.

¹²[c]For our sons are like saplings,
   well-tended in their youth;
   our daughters are like cornerstones
   trimmed to give shape to a palace.
¹³Our storehouses are full,
   supplying produce of all kinds;
   our flocks number thousands,
   even myriads, in our fields;
   ¹⁴our cattle are well cared for.
There is no breaching and no sortie,
   and no wailing in our streets.

¹⁵Happy the people who have it so;
   happy the people whose God is the LORD.

ᵃ *So Targum, Saadia; others "my people."*
ᵇ *With Rashi; lit. "right hand."*
ᶜ *The meaning of several phrases in vv. 12–14 is uncertain.*

171

145 A song of praise. Of David.

א   I will extol You, my God and king,
        and bless Your name forever and ever.

ב   ²Every day will I bless You
        and praise Your name forever and ever.

ג   ³Great is the LORD and much acclaimed;
        His greatness cannot be fathomed.

ד   ⁴One generation shall laud Your works to another
        and declare Your mighty acts.

ה   ⁵The glorious majesty of Your splendor
        ᵃ⁻and Your wondrous acts⁻ᵃ will I recite.

ו   ⁶Men shall talk of the might of Your awesome deeds,
        and I will recount Your greatness.

ז   ⁷They shall celebrate Your abundant goodness,
        and sing joyously of Your beneficence.

ח   ⁸The LORD is gracious and compassionate,
        slow to anger and abounding in kindness.

ט   ⁹The LORD is good to all,
        and His mercy is upon all His works.

י   ¹⁰All Your works shall praise You, O LORD,
        and Your faithful ones shall bless You.

כ   ¹¹They shall talk of the majesty of Your kingship,
        and speak of Your might,

ל   ¹²to make His mighty acts known among men
        and the majestic glory of His kingship.

מ   ¹³Your kingship is an eternal kingship;
        Your dominion is for all generations.

ס   ¹⁴The LORD supports all who stumble,
        and makes all who are bent stand straight.

ע   ¹⁵The eyes of all look to You expectantly,
        and You give them their food when it is due.

פ   ¹⁶You give it openhandedly,
        feeding every creature to its heart's content.

צ   ¹⁷The LORD is beneficent in all His ways
        and faithful in all His works.

ק   ¹⁸The LORD is near to all who call Him,

ᵃ⁻ᵃ *A Qumran Ps. scroll reads: "they will speak of, and Your wonders."*

to all who call Him with sincerity.

ר 19He fulfills the wishes of those who fear Him;
He hears their cry and delivers them.

שׁ 20The LORD watches over all who love Him,
but all the wicked He will destroy.

ת 21My mouth shall utter the praise of the LORD,
and all creaturesᵇ shall bless His holy name forever and ever.

146 Hallelujah.

Praise the LORD, O my soul!
2I will praise the LORD all my life,
sing hymns to my God while I exist.

3Put not your trust in the great,
in mortal man who cannot save.
4His breath departs;
he returns to the dust;
on that day his plans come to nothing.

5Happy is he who has the God of Jacob for his help,
whose hope is in the LORD his God,
6maker of heaven and earth,
the sea and all that is in them;
who keeps faith forever;
7who secures justice for those who are wronged,
gives food to the hungry.
The LORD sets prisoners free;
8The LORD restores sight to the blind;
the LORD makes those who are bent stand straight;
the LORD loves the righteous;
9The LORD watches over the stranger;
He gives courage to the orphan and widow,
but makes the path of the wicked tortuous.

10The LORD shall reign forever,
your God, O Zion, for all generations.
Hallelujah.

ᵇ Lit. *"flesh."*

147 Hallelujah.

It is good to chant hymns to our God;
    it is pleasant to sing glorious praise.

2The LORD rebuilds Jerusalem;
    He gathers in the exiles of Israel.
3He heals their broken hearts,
    and binds up their wounds.
4He reckoned the number of the stars;
    to each He gave its name.
5Great is our LORD and full of power;
    His wisdom is beyond reckoning.
6The LORD gives courage to the lowly,
    and brings the wicked down to the dust.

7Sing to the LORD a song of praise,
    chant a hymn with a lyre to our God,
      8who covers the heavens with clouds,
    provides rain for the earth,
    makes mountains put forth grass;
      9who gives the beasts their food,
    to the raven's brood what they cry for.
10He does not prize the strength of horses,
    nor value the fleetness[a] of men;
      11but the LORD values those who fear Him,
    those who depend on His faithful care.

12O Jerusalem, glorify the LORD;
    praise your God, O Zion!
13For He made the bars of your gates strong,
    and blessed your children within you.
14He endows your realm with well-being,
    and satisfies you with choice wheat.

15He sends forth His word to the earth;
    His command runs swiftly.
16He lays down snow like fleece,
    scatters frost like ashes.
17He tosses down hail like crumbs—

---

a Lit. "thigh."

who can endure His icy cold?
¹⁸He issues a command—it melts them;
He breathes—the waters flow.
¹⁹He issued His commands to Jacob,
His statutes and rules to Israel.
²⁰He did not do so for any other nation;
of such rules they know nothing.
Hallelujah.

148 Hallelujah.

Praise the LORD from the heavens;
praise Him on high.
²Praise Him, all His angels,
praise Him, all His hosts.
³Praise Him, sun and moon,
praise Him, all bright stars.
⁴Praise Him, highest heavens,
and you waters that are above the heavens.
⁵Let them praise the name of the LORD,
for it was He who commanded that they be created.
⁶He made them endure forever,
establishing an order that shall never change.
⁷Praise the LORD, O you who are on earth,
all sea monsters and ocean depths,
⁸fire and hail, snow and smoke,
storm wind that executes His command,
⁹all mountains and hills,
all fruit trees and cedars,
¹⁰all wild and tamed beasts,
creeping things and winged birds,
¹¹all kings and peoples of the earth,
all princes of the earth and its judges,
¹²youths and maidens alike,
old and young together.
¹³Let them praise the name of the LORD,
for His name, His alone, is sublime;
His splendor covers heaven and earth.
¹⁴He has exalted the horn of His people
for the glory of all His faithful ones,

Israel, the people close to Him.
Hallelujah.

149 Hallelujah.

Sing to the LORD a new song,
His praises in the congregation of the faithful.
²Let Israel rejoice in its maker;
let the children of Zion exult in their king.
³Let them praise His name in dance;
with timbrel and lyre let them chant His praises.
⁴For the LORD delights in His people;
He adorns the lowly with victory.
⁵Let the faithful exult in glory;
let them shout for joy upon their couches,
⁶with paeans to God in their throats
and two-edged swords in their hands,
⁷to impose retribution upon the nations,
punishment upon the peoples,
⁸binding their kings with shackles,
their nobles with chains of iron,
⁹executing the doom decreed against them.
This is the glory of all His faithful.
Hallelujah.

150 Hallelujah.

Praise God in His sanctuary;
praise Him in the sky, His stronghold.
²Praise Him for His mighty acts;
praise Him forª His exceeding greatness.
³Praise Him with blasts of the horn;
praise Him with harp and lyre.
⁴Praise Him with timbrel and dance;
praise Him with lute and pipe.
⁵Praise Him with resounding cymbals;
praise Him with loud-clashing cymbals.
⁶Let all that breathes praise the LORD.
Hallelujah.

ª Or "as befits."

Meditations

Meditations

Meditations

Meditations

Meditations

Meditations

Meditations

Meditations

Meditations

Meditations

Meditations

Meditations

Meditations

Meditations

Meditations

Meditations

Meditations

Meditations

Meditations

Meditations

Meditations

Meditations

Meditations

Meditations